"Andrew Farley's books have had a huge impact on my spiritual life, challenging me to live an authentic, grace-filled life. *Operation Screwtape* is his most entertaining work yet. Once you start reading this book, you won't want to put it down!"

Bart Millard, lead singer for MercyMe

"*Operation Screwtape* channels the creativity and wit of C. S. Lewis while introducing the brilliant insights Andrew Farley is already known for in his bestselling books. This book will entertain you, but it will also challenge you to awaken to some astounding realities that, apparently, the forces of darkness will do anything to hide."

David Gregory, *New York Times* bestselling author of *Dinner with a Perfect Stranger*

OPERATION
SCREWTAPE

OPERATION
SCREWTAPE

THE ART OF SPIRITUAL WAR

ANDREW FARLEY

BakerBooks

a division of Baker Publishing Group
Grand Rapids, Michigan

© 2012 by Andrew Farley

Published by Baker Books
a division of Baker Publishing Group
P.O. Box 6287, Grand Rapids, MI 49516-6287
www.bakerbooks.com

Printed in the United States of America

Library of Congress Cataloging-in-Publication Data
Farley, Andrew, 1972–
    Operation Screwtape : the art of spiritual war / Andrew Farley.
       p.   cm.
    ISBN 978-0-8010-1447-5 (cloth)
       1. Devil—Christianity—Miscellanea. 2. Spiritual warfare—Miscellanea.
    3. Christianity—Controversial literature. I. Title.
    BT982.F37 2012
    235′.4—dc23   2012028046

This is a work of fiction. Names, characters, incidents, and dialogues are products of the author's imagination and are not to be construed as real. Any resemblance to actual events or persons, living or dead, is entirely coincidental.

The internet addresses, email addresses, and phone numbers in this book are accurate at the time of publication. They are provided as a resource. Baker Publishing Group does not endorse them or vouch for their content or permanence.

In keeping with biblical principles of creation stewardship, Baker Publishing Group advocates the responsible use of our natural resources. As a member of the Green Press Initiative, our company uses recycled paper when possible. The text paper of this book is composed in part of post-consumer waste.

Published in association with the literary agency of Alive Communications, Inc., 7680 Goddard Street, Suite 200, Colorado Springs, CO 80920, alivecommunications.com.

12 13 14 15 16 17 18   7 6 5 4 3 2 1

In memory of Clive Staples Lewis,
the first to document their existence

Contents

Preface

It should soon be obvious why I cannot provide detail when it comes to the discovery of the document you hold in your hand. My colleague and I argued for nearly five months before I consented to release the footage of our discovery on the internet. At this point, what is done is done, and there is no turning back.

The fact that Deputy Director Meyerriecks and her staff would come in and take what is rightfully my property and then go so far as to deny its very existence compelled me to release this to the public. While I was willing to work "within the system," as they phrased it, it has now become quite clear that they have no intention of including me in their affairs. They simply used me to get what they wanted.

Admittedly, when they first inquired, I did tell them that I had not made any copies of any files, and that was not entirely truthful of me. Nevertheless, given the Agency's actions as of late, I feel that I am well within my rights to release this.

I want to express gratitude to my publisher for their willingness to support me in the publication of this work. If anything should happen to me as a result, I have taken measures to ensure that one way or another, the work itself will be available to the public for many years to come.

About This Translation

Having taught numerous graduate-level linguistics courses pertaining to the many languages of the world—their phonology, morphology, and syntax—and having worked on countless translation projects, I can say without any hesitation that this is like nothing I have seen before.

I have taken a phrasal (rather than word-level) approach to translation, as I found the morphosyntax in general to be radically different from the characteristics of our human languages. Nevertheless, the principal ideas are conveyed as accurately as possible, given the constraints of the English language.

I should also admit that in just a few cases of lexical or semantic ambiguity, I could not determine with absolute certainty what the writer intended to communicate. Given the contextual clues in each case, I made the best educated guess possible. Of course, if there are any errors in translation, all responsibility for those errors is exclusively mine.

I do not consider myself to be an expert on otherworldliness, and while it is obvious that this is some sort of manual of conduct, I have decided to present it to you just as it came into my possession. I have not included any commentary on the text, nor am I certain that I should. The document speaks for itself, and there is no need for my personal biases to enter in and skew your own interpretation of what you read here. As this document reaches the public, others may feel more qualified to comment with their interpretations or to supply background information for some of what is found here.

Note that certain fixed expressions such as "the Work," "the One," "the Life," and "the Ghost" carried a diminutive marker of sorts—they literally appeared smaller than the rest of the text in the document. It seemed to be a way to belittle the concepts. Although I have not reproduced the diminutive effect here, I want you to be aware that it was present in the original file.

It may be of interest to the reader to know that there were millions, maybe billions, of other files archived and "interlinked" (for lack of a better term) on the device. However, I was only able to copy this, the largest file, before Deputy Director Meyerriecks seized the device. I cannot speculate on the contents of the other, smaller files, but it seemed that each was marked with its own case number.

What follows is only the information found on the master file in the order in which it appeared.

Introduction

Any master deceiver knows that sound intelligence is the foundation for a victorious operation. Our most successful tactics have always been formulated in light of research we conducted through prior contact. With that in mind, this guide offers the novice tempter a collection of our most current approaches.

You are undoubtedly aware of the rise and fall of our senior colleague Screwtape, as well as the brainless blunders of those once under his tutelage. Given the way events have unfolded as of late, we felt it most advantageous to systematically educate young tempters as early as possible rather than to lose many of them to the same fiery fate to which we lost Screwtape.

With this goal in mind, we present *Operation Screwtape*, a combat manual designed to train you in the art of spiritual war. We have thoughtfully titled this compilation in order to imprint on your devious little minds a reminder that you too might suffer along with the one you once idolized should you fail to heed the guidelines herein. In short, learn or burn.

We realize that strategies must allow for some flexibility based on what is needed at a precise moment in the field. Regardless, we expect you to maintain the highest standards in your work, as it is both your expertise and your ability to adapt faster than your opponent that will determine whether you succeed or fail.

If you adhere to the principles outlined herein, you will find your efforts duly rewarded. However, should you fail to heed these principles and in so doing hurt our cause in the slightest, you will suffer the proper punishment. After all, if one is purposefully or even accidentally insubordinate to Our Father Below, what should one expect other than that we inflict on that one what is due?

Now, what you find here is the accumulated wisdom of our foremost experts in this area of study. From these myriad experiences, newer operants glean significant knowledge and spare themselves the countless vain efforts already made by those who went out before them. Keep in mind that these are general constructs, and the foundational principles are the same for every form of deception we launch. Our principal goal is to inundate patients with subtly incompatible belief systems such that we obscure the simple truth about the Life. We could introduce you to a slew of ignorant creatures upon whom our methods have been most effective.

Note also that this manual is required reading during the first millennium of study at the House of Correction for Incompetent Tempters. For those deceivers who once fancied themselves as being in the know, undoubtedly you will realize there have been radical improvements in combat over the last century or two, as traditional temptations have often been found insufficient to dislodge a patient from his contented position. This is all the more reason that our most current stratagems must remain confidential and go unnoticed. The only thing more advantageous than the patients not knowing our methods is for them to believe they actually *do* know our methods. Currently, the majority of them only believe us to be horned devils tempting them to do evil. Let us work together to both surprise and bewilder them.

dragon principle 1

STEAL

1

00010111+/00001000010111000011110/100010./10·0:01011/10001101000+011101000101110000110/1000|0. 1110001011100011-101000000

Steal Influence

e begin our discussion of strategies with the case of patients who still live within our magnificent darkness. Perhaps something has piqued their interest to the point that they are willing, even eager, to entertain the thought of becoming a child of the Enemy. But one fact always works in our favor: hypocrisy is repulsive to them. The bipeds flee from it as if escaping the foulest of odors. We witness this phenomenon often, as the church is considered by many to be the ultimate embodiment of two-facedness. They speak of love yet go on backbiting.

They speak of forgiveness yet wallow in bitterness and shame. They even speak now and then of the Work itself yet seldom act like it is real.

Those who belong to us can smell their hypocrisy from such a distance that they have no desire to approach the scene, much less inquire of anything substantive. As long as the church is centered on the feeble proclamation of moral principles and ethical standards, we will maintain momentum in casting them as hypocrites. Today's prominent messages of behavior modification and self-improvement within the Body breed the very accusations of hypocrisy they work to dispel. And when they are blinded by us to the way of the Work, they cannot begin to fathom where they err.

Highlight Hypocrisy

When dealing with those who belong to us, it is critical, of course, that you channel their attention toward the hypocrisy that riddles the Body. Introduce them to those who say one thing and do another, and then warn them to be careful, to self-protect, in order not to be swindled or taken in by those who are only fakers, or fools at best.

Make it your chief aim to focus them on the weaknesses within the Body. Have them believe that the church on the whole is broken and devoid of authenticity. If you put into the forefront of their minds the inevitable flaws found among church messengers, you will find that the message itself is then discredited. And once you construct the convincing argument that a perfect deity would never allow such imperfection in his own church, seekers of truth will inevitably move on, perhaps to one of our respectable religions, as they resume their fruitless search for perfection.

Of course, this strategy will still fail when it comes to *some* who seek truth. They may indeed take notice of hypocrisy within the church yet show themselves willing to look past it. What then? At this point, there is only one sensible move to make: you must obscure the message, keeping it clouded at all costs, and appeal to their fleshly appetites for any tantalizing alternative.

For example, direct them to perceive the church as a source of reform, a way to improve or refresh their *current* life rather than to exchange it for an altogether different one. Induce them to see it merely as a means to make acquaintances and socialize with a community of relatively moral people. Busy them with programs and service commitments. All of this is harmless, as long as we do not permit them to take notice of the Life.

Pressure Tactics

Now, concerning evangelism, some of their own do the work for us as they fixate on obtaining a nearly instantaneous decision from unsuspecting and uninformed victims of their assault. The overt pressure applied by their "boldest" evangelists seems to yield few real converts, and many of their targets resist because they find the whole ordeal repulsive. Some even find themselves angered by the brash, impersonal measures designed to manipulate them into response. Of course, this translates into benefit for us as those same targets are only more difficult to reach upon their next attempt.

There is always the slim possibility that their target responds to the evangelistic appeal. But even this is by no means reason to despair. With such urgency placed on saying their magical words as a rote prayer, the victim of their vile sales pitch may walk away with very little to go on. Yes, he has repeated various phrases which, if truly meant in his heart, could result in birth and therefore be dangerous to our cause. Still, in many cases (more than you might think!), the true effect of their noisy, impersonal approach pales in comparison to the methods we once observed in the early church.

There was a more difficult time when the Body understood that our subjects would only be converted through hearing with faith. When this reality was taken into account, many subjects took personal interest in their harmonious love for one another and then gained exposure to the Work over days or weeks, even months or years. They heard a comprehensive message and thereby came to believe apart from pressure tactics or induced decisions. The result was a solid foundation that sprang from time and exposure rather than the shallow introductions we witness today when their so-called evangelists roll into town, fire off several rounds of gospel ammunition, and then head for the airport.

If leaders within the Body are willing to settle for this form of evangelism, then so are we. We do well to tolerate their quick-decision technique and their formulaic prayers. In this way, we keep many of our own safe from the Enemy, and the Work remains foggy at best.

Additionally, if everything is going well, these pressure tactics are then portrayed to the masses as the only proper and dedicated form of evangelism. The majority of them will quietly lose heart as they naturally lack the brash personality needed to go confidently storming in. At this point, we inflict significant wounds through accusation. We simply exploit their feelings of fear and inferiority, such that they file themselves away as second-class citizens in the kingdom. We present them with the nearly undeniable fact that they are either unwilling or unable to "count the cost" and "pay the price," as their own teachers like to put it. Like clockwork, their self-evaluation is followed by their self-condemnation. This always brings a smile to our faces.

2

Steal Security

e know that once a patient has believed in the Work to the point of death, metamorphosis, and inhabitation, that process cannot under any circumstances be reversed. It may surprise you to learn, however, that the patients themselves do not all see it so clearly. So while they may be lost to us forever, we can prevent them from realizing their secure position. We can still induce them to expend enormous emotional capital working to maintain what they already possess.

To foment fear, play on a patient's sense of insecurity. Provoke him to panic at the idea that the very salvation he once received may now be in jeopardy, hanging in the balance. Heap an undeniable sense of anguish upon him. Haunt him constantly with the many sins he has committed. And of course, harp on the one past sin that particularly worries him or, alternatively, the recurring one that continually trips him up.

It is important that you not only move faster than your opponent but also move smarter. In this regard, we can even use some of their teachers—those who amusingly fail to embrace the fullness of the Work—to reinforce our efforts. Convince these leaders that it is surely their sworn duty to warn that any willful sin at all keeps their followers from their inheritance and may change their eternal destiny altogether.

Special Cases

In some cases, a patient has been so isolated from immorality that he cannot imagine himself to have committed any act heinous enough to cause him to lose his place. He measures his sins and concludes they are not sufficiently weighty. In this case, no amount of accusation about his past will have effect. Here the best method is to undermine his sense of security by bolstering his belief that some sins are weightier than others. Then, with this planted in his mind, shift his focus away from his past and toward the hypothetical of what he *might* do in the future: *What if I despair and commit suicide? What if my marriage ends in divorce? What if I begin to doubt my faith?* It makes no difference which of these hypothetical questions serves to build a hint of fear in him. As long as he remains devoted to some sort of measuring of sins, he will not see the Work in all of its despicable glory, nor will he find any justifiable reason to celebrate his security.

In reality, of course, it makes no difference which sins the children of the Enemy happen to commit. We know that *all* their sins have been taken away, once and for all. The only act that places any of their race in jeopardy is the sin of unbelief in the Work itself. And once they believe to the point of crossing over from death into the Life, they are eternally lost to us. Still, for all practical purposes, the reality of their secure position remains concealed during the course of their time on Earth as we effectively persuade them that sins, whether big ones or small ones in accumulated succession, cause them to lose connection with the Ghost. In this way, we turn the Message into a behavior-centered dogma that so stimulates a hyper-consciousness of sins that nearly any patient can be confused about where he stands.

At first, repeating salvation prayers now and then may bring him comfort. However, as we return to heap more guilt, even that sanctuary comes crashing down. He begins the cycle of feeling distant and dirty, praying to be re-saved, feeling confident once again, and then having his hopes dashed as the feelings fade and our accusation ensues. He spirals toward inevitable demise.

Note in all of this that the patient's attention is deflected away from the truth of the Work. He is fixated on, if not entirely obsessed with, his own self-assessment. At this juncture few bring themselves to consider the oath made between the Enemy and Himself to preserve them for all eternity. This seems a distant theological notion at best. Instead, the typical patient finds himself consumed with his own sins, not the Enemy's promise, and he is wholly defeated. This is how, if we are persistent, the tiny flame of insecurity can be fanned into a blazing fire of self-condemnation.

A Doctrine of Doubt

There are steps we can take to propagate this con-demnation beyond the individual level and reach the masses. But as we mentioned earlier, it can only happen as their leaders perpetuate our doctrines. In this way we leverage *their* influence to reach *our* goals. In this section we outline a most compelling doctrine that simultaneously obscures the Work from those of our own possession and incites alarm in the children of the Enemy.

We begin with the obvious truth. The very act of salvation itself means that a subject has died and risen. He receives a new human spirit and a new heart. He is for the first time capable of obedience from the heart, as the Ghost himself has inscribed his desires within his offspring. Consequently, the One *is* both his Savior and Lord by default, as the patient was raised to newness of life under the lord-ship of the One. Nevertheless, we find it possible to skew this reality, twisting his lordship into a work *the patient* must persistently manage.

At first glance, it might seem counterproductive that we teach a patient to "make" or "keep" the One as Lord of his life. After all, isn't this the polar opposite of what we want? In actuality, our research department has concluded that splitting the One's role "as Savior" from his role "as Lord" serves us well in the acquisition of territory. So before you judge this approach prematurely, permit us to illustrate the point and deepen your learning.

Assume we train a recent convert to "make" and "keep" the One as Lord of his life. Perhaps he sees the situation much like a car with two steering wheels. We persuade him that he must continually choose to let go of the wheel (deny himself) and let the One drive, apart from him. Should he fail to do so, it inevitably brings into question whether he was truly saved at the start. (Note that some pitiful specimens will even imagine they have somehow tossed the frail author of their salvation into the backseat!)

By constantly working to make the Enemy his Lord, over and over, the patient is blinded to the reality that the Enemy is already his Lord since the Enemy birthed him as his own offspring, obedient from the heart. The patient fails to see that the Enemy firmly placed his children within the kingdom of which he is *already* King.

Our perfectly twisted doctrinal offering places the focus squarely on the patient and his ability to peel his fingers off the steering wheel of his life. Give such importance to this issue that it clouds the truth about believing and fixing his gaze on the One and his Work. Let him doubt he has properly received the Life if he has not matched his receiving with an equal part of doing. If we leave him to make this judgment call, we keep him wondering whether or not his salvation ever genuinely took root. In the midst of his infancy in the One, he will begin doubting he was ever born!

With this newfound belief system, he plummets into the world of introspection and self-evaluation, right where we want him. Doubts concerning lordship easily become questions about his own commitment. Questions about commitment lead to wondering about salvation itself: *Did I devote myself to him completely? Did I give all of myself? Did I really surrender to his lordship? Am I truly saved?*

If the patient feels the Enemy might not yet be "fully" Lord of his life, he will naturally seek to accumulate enough evidence of his own conversion. This performance mentality, accompanied by the inevitable self-inspection, breeds beautiful questions like the aforementioned. With these doubts constantly looming over him, we pour on the fear that so wonderfully accompanies them, snaring the convert in a consuming self-focus, all under a "lordship" label.

In all of this, the patient looks to his own commitment and is blinded to the One's everlasting devotion to him. He is consumed with fabricating a form of life to offer rather than celebrating the Life he freely received. He envisions the Enemy as one who responds to his level of initiative, not realizing the Enemy freely gives him all good things. And as he wallows in unwarranted despair, *we* are the ones who are more than conquerors.

3

0001011l+/00001000101ll 0000ll10/100010 /10/0l0l0ll/l000ll010000+0lll0l000l0ll/00001ll0/l000l0..1llu000l0llll0000ll-l0l000u00

Steal Intimacy

he forgiveness conferred upon these children of the Enemy came at the price of the Blood. And we know that what is sealed in blood can never be canceled out. So what are we to do in this case except cloud the truth? As is often the case, it seems their weakness lies in their lack of understanding.

The High Command has issued a mandate that at all costs, we must not let them comprehend the Blood. This is both a great responsibility and a most delicate task. We must distract them with any appealing alternative, coaxing them to seek another means to forgiveness. We dim their awareness by training them to exchange one currency for another, substituting any form of recompense in place of the Blood.

One most enticing substitute is the apology, also known as the confession or the asking of forgiveness—any word-driven means of obtaining forgiveness. This is an approach they already use with one another. They often forgive only when the offender realizes his error and initiates restoration with an apology. This quaint exchange eventually returns the offender to his former state within the relationship. Therefore, human forgiveness requires a series of actions taken by the offender, and there is no blood transaction. This concept is deeply embedded within their societies, and many victories have been achieved by having patients imagine the Enemy operates in this manner.

Of course, the Book announces their forgiveness as purchased in blood more than two millennia ago. In no way does it depend on any ongoing action of their own. Nothing they say or do contributes to what has already been done on their behalf. But because they are accustomed to the human exchange of verbal apologies to restore broken relationships, we find we can nearly effortlessly distract them with their own familiar notion. We simply introduce the idea that their relationship with the Enemy is broken, that their fellowship with his Ghost is disrupted, or even that their prayers are not heard or answered when they have any current struggle with sin (which, if we succeed in other areas, translates into every day of their miserable lives!).

We call this the Separation Principle.

The Separation Principle

Note that each deception we present carries both *form* and *content*. Form is the packaging, while content is the message itself. The form in which the Separation Principle is packaged is every bit as important as its content. Novice tempter, you cannot afford for your efforts to fail because you did not appeal to a patient through both.

The key to success here is to present the doctrine in a form that appeals to the desire every sensible human rightly possesses: the desire for good standing before the Enemy. Here we make sure they are occupied with this most important "spiritual" concern, inducing them to rush about seeking to get right and stay right; to get forgiven and stay forgiven; to get cleansed and stay cleansed. In so doing, they do not see the all-encompassing nature of the forgiveness they already possess in the One.

We convince them that when they commit sins, this creates a rift between them and the Enemy. They are deluded into believing that the Ghost has abandoned them or withdrawn himself, whether to a realm just above them, where he hovers, or to heaven itself, from which he must be beckoned to bring them salvation anew. Note that some fail to equate possession of the Ghost with salvation itself. Hence, they are quite open to the absurd notion that they might still possess one (salvation) while forfeiting the other (the Ghost) when any sin is committed.

In this way, we are able to apply significant pressure to the patient, since the Separation Principle masquerades as a disciplinary measure from the Enemy. Few patients look far enough ahead to realize it will lead to all manner of anxiety as their sins, both those remembered and those forgotten, inevitably accumulate over time. Their sense of distance from the One only snowballs as they compare their performance with that of others and feel as if they are drifting farther and farther away. Alternatively, some envision a vertical scale of intimacy with the One, and due to their besetting sins, imagine themselves diving downward.

Falling from Fellowship

One of our initial goals is to move patients to believe their salvation itself is in jeopardy. But many will not journey so far with us. Still, studies reveal that these may readily allow that their "fellowship" is in danger. Of course, it is their fellowship, their enduring connection with the Ghost, that is the power for change in their lives.

When, in light of their many sins, they grow uncertain about the permanence of the Ghost, they find themselves immobilized and helpless. And once they have invested fully in our fellowship doctrine, we simply make every effort to keep a sin struggle of any sort current in their lives and thereby eliminate any hope of confident connection with the Enemy (or any perceived answers to prayer, for that matter). Their imagined condition serves as their penance—a penance from which they can never escape!

If they naïvely concede to the idea that their relationship with the Enemy is contingent upon their memory, their confession, and their promises to act differently in the future, we gain significant ground. At this point they lose sight of their one and only means of forgiveness—the Blood. In its place, they substitute a weak and worthless attempt to get cleansed over and over, a method even deadlier than the old way of the law itself. (Recall that at least under the law, the sons and daughters of Moses made their temple trek only once a *year* to be forgiven. But these pathetic creatures of today settle for a "mental cleansing" that must occur not yearly but, even worse, on a sin-by-sin basis. Without a doubt, it keeps them occupied!)

By whatever means necessary, we must root out any thought that their fellowship is stable and secure. Keep their minds away from the reality that even when they are faithless, the Enemy remains faithful. Do not let them perceive the closeness they possess—that they are one spirit with him. Distort the fellowship they have with the Ghost and keep everything hazy in their minds. Otherwise, they will be empowered to live from the Life.

Bring them to such a condition that they see themselves as the sum total of their recent sins. Then when they are caught in a sin, they will sense little or no impetus for change. At this point, impress on them the idea that they have been left alone to resolve the struggle and get right with their deity. According to our observations, they will not be conscious of our influence, and by the time they are, it will be too late in most cases. After we have trained them in the belief that they are growing more and more distant from the Enemy as sins accrue, the thought of applying a gracious, once-for-all forgiveness to their situation will seem to them like licentious heresy.

Inducing Paralysis

Taken to an extreme, the idea that a patient's own forgiveness depends on himself can nearly paralyze him. All his attention shifts to reviewing and tracking and apologizing for every sin he has recently committed. Picture one of their computers when a process hangs there, incomplete: nothing else functions well while the one process remains in motion, using all the resources. Work hard to ensure this mental tallying takes over a patient's mind, and his sins, not his Savior, will become his obsession.

Bring out all the evidence against him. Keep his mind on his performance record. Aggravate him by pouring on the guilt. In this way, you set him up for a treadmill experience of "sin, confess, get cleansed, sin, confess, get cleansed." You push him toward self-focus, self-inspection, and ultimately self-reliance, whether he realizes it or not.

If you find that your influence is waning, redouble your efforts with new tactics. Remember that tradition stifles innovation, so do not allow yourself to settle into a repetitive pattern of monotonous accusation if it yields no fruit. Adaptation is key. Further assessment of a situation usually reveals how one can increase productivity and gain territory.

Whatever it takes, do not let a patient understand the Blood, as our situation would indeed become desperate. The most heinous truth he could possibly come to realize is that he has all of the Ghost, all of the time, no matter what. None of this can be allowed to enter his mind; we must get it out of him entirely. He must be encouraged to believe that he may only experience a portion of the Ghost, and only some of the time, and only during those times in which his recent performance has been adequate and his feelings confirm it. We cannot allow him to choose apart from his feelings, and we cannot permit him to believe apart from his own self-assessments.

Conclusion

In sum, as we drive patients to look toward human relationships for proper perspective on relating to the Enemy, they will equate the earthly with the heavenly. They will fail to see the Blood in all its glory.

We know that they have been called, by the very Work they supposedly honor, into pure and unbreakable fellowship that *should* seem to them even more present in the midst of a struggle. After all, it is that same fellowship with the Ghost that empowers them to say no to our schemes. Nevertheless, we find that they are indeed willing to lend us their ears, allowing us to mold and shape their beliefs about forgiveness, cleansing, fellowship, and nearly any matter involving the Work. The immense responsibility thrust upon us is that of persistently accusing them, both day and night. In our view, there is no greater pleasure under the sun.

4

Steal Clarity

e have seen how profitable it can be to offer patients the idea that their forgiveness depends on their own actions. As we dig into the core of this stratagem, we identify a corollary idea to further perpetuate: that forgiveness is an *ongoing* process. Here we spark in them the sense that they are progressively being forgiven as they penitently request it. The image we like them to seize upon is that the Enemy is continually "zapping" them with new portions of cleansing as they repent and plead for it.

Repeating any action over time develops a habit. You should keep this in mind as you train them to only feel forgiven when they have carried out the right measures. In the shorter term, this belief system may bring them the confirming feelings of forgiveness they seek. However, over the long term the belief system will indeed betray them. Hampered by feelings of doubt about whether they have taken *all* the proper steps concerning *all* the right sins, they will succumb to the bewilderment we produce in them. In this way, we strip them of any enduring confidence and darken their conscience.

A Heaven-Earth Dichotomy

Never underestimate the effect of complicating a matter. Humans love to obtain "knowledge" and then lord it over others. So when we introduce an intellectually entertaining twist on the Work, they leap on it. Some of them even take things further than we do, twisting the Message in inventive ways that we in turn use against other patients!

When it comes to the message of the Blood, train them in a false dichotomy. They are easily swayed toward a perceived division between what is true on earth versus what is valid in heaven.

While living on earth and awaiting his heavenly body, a patient may feel that anything in the "heavenly" category is far off, irrelevant to his present life. Therefore, we induce him to conclude he has total forgiveness only in a heavenly and "positional" sense, rather than an actual free pardon in the here and now. This double-talk carries the appearance of esteeming the Book's passages on total forgiveness but still supplies us ample room to inundate the patient with guilt, which humans take to in their morbid, religious sort of way. You will thoroughly enjoy the spectacle.

Along these lines, steer the dimwit toward a parallel notion that there are two sets of record books: a heavenly bookkeeping in accord with the Work and an earthly bookkeeping in which sins have not yet been dealt with. This deception yields considerable effects as heavenly bookkeeping brings no practical benefit for daily living. This trains the patient to feel obligated to keep up his end in dealing with his sins "on earth," where he resides each and every day of his life. This breeds an infatuation with sins, obscuring the Work.

Note that even the old way of the law provided yearly relief from guilt, a forgiveness enjoyed right on their planet via the *blood* of bulls and goats alone. How absurd it is for any patient today under the Enemy's new way to believe that his forgiveness is not real, actual, and "once for all," even as the Book proclaims. After all, does not the Blood of the One actually cleanse them more than the sacrifices of old?

Nevertheless, we can and do persuade them that the Blood only cleanses them in some heavenly, progressive, or future sense not yet fully realized. Herein, we weaken the Work in their eyes, limiting its effects to heaven alone. As patients buy into our approach, they insult the Ghost and put the Work to shame.

Although we have presented effective strategies for guarding patients from a true understanding of forgiveness, there are some not afflicted by even our wiliest schemes. What can be done if they begin to realize the all-encompassing power of the Blood? Do not despair, as there is one final measure we can employ.

The Final Measure

Patients who discover and more fully honor the blood currency are not a lost cause, as there is still opportunity to gain leverage. But if sporadic action is taken at this point without proper study and assessment, then both time and energy are wasted with nothing to show for it. Fortunately, our Research Department informs us that in cases like these, a crafty agent can still suppress a full understanding of the Work.

Our findings indicate that patients with some level of understanding are still open to the silly notion that their sins are merely "covered." Unknowingly, they equate the Blood under the Enemy's new way with that of animal blood under the old way. Of course, this subtly allows for the possibility that there might be more to cover at some point, or that somehow sins might get uncovered, resurfacing to a visible state.

A psychological advantage is secured with this bait-and-switch element. We simply exchange one view of forgiveness for another. In this way, we have rescued many situations that at first seemed hopeless. If they perceive their sins to still be there, only covered, they are more likely to preoccupy themselves with those sins. It is only those who realize that their sins are completely removed and that they need not have consciousness of them who truly take hold of the message about the Blood. So we do whatever we can to further both the language and the concept of covering.

We cannot permit their thoughts to gravitate toward the one-time removal of their sins; nor the truth that the One remembers them no more; nor that the Ghost living within them also testifies concerning the sufficiency of the Blood. If they discover these truths and grasp them with clarity, they will commit themselves to living in the present, no longer enmeshed in a morass of the past. They will look outside themselves toward others and even begin to, dare we say it, love. Should this occur, the battle with these freaks has already seen its best days.

5

00010111+0000100010111000011101100010.010/0.0101011/10001101000040111010001011100001110100010.11100010111000011-101000000

Steal Confidence

Some who are well grounded in the Work can still be moved to embrace ambiguity when it comes to the Day of Judgment. If you weigh on them with the idea that they will be held accountable—judged for their sins one day—you cast a shadow on their understanding and incite fear. Yes, even when they have believed in the Blood and counted on it for salvation from consuming fires, you still attain a position of strength over them once they begin entertaining the concept of a sin judgment. Here you use an uncertain future to your benefit, imploring them to await the return of their Lord and Judge with a suitable degree of "godly fear." This hinders them from confidently and eagerly awaiting his return. The impending judgment they imagine blinds them to his loathsome Love that should cast away all their concern.

Fear of the future impacts the present. By projecting the image of future judgment on the canvas of their minds, you introduce confusion and ultimately breed panic. Sure, they nod their heads at the notion of the Enemy remembering their sins no more, but they are still quite willing to believe he will recall their sins once again on Judgment Day. Although the blatant contradiction is more than apparent to us, these buffoons simply do not register their own double-mindedness. Hence, the Work is perceived as powerless due to the haze we pour over them.

The Rewards Scheme

Not every patient is susceptible to this ploy. But we do find those who rightly object to accountability for sins on the Day of Judgment may still entertain the possibility that their *good* deeds will be quantified and measured for an equivalent awarding of wealth.

I realize how preposterous this sounds, but never undervalue their affinity for material possessions and public adulation.

Of course, the grain of truth here is that they will indeed receive the crown of life and a vast inheritance in the One. But this reward concept can be perverted, spurring them to collect "credits" which they believe will be exchanged for heavenly loot. To those who tend toward self-degradation, we whisper that this point system will one day expose them as second-class citizens in the kingdom, not worthy of as much material wealth as their peers. For those more confident in the flesh, we drive them to live for a future material gain, inflating their minds with pride as they assess their performance and anticipate greater wealth and status.

This judgment-rewards scheme diverts focus away from the One and the Work. Motivation for doing good no longer stems from a heart freely desiring to keep in step with the Ghost and naturally overflowing with joy. Instead, we exploit the fleshly desire for riches by promoting a heavenly booty they believe they are earning or—equally helpful—failing to earn.

It makes no difference whether a patient excels or falls short in his own mind. Those who see themselves as not making the grade succumb to a self-loathing as they compare themselves to others. They can be harassed. Meanwhile, those who do well in their own estimation can learn pride. Either way, we win. In the same way that we have sidelined some of our own subjects by coaxing them to chase after upper levels of paradise or more virgins in the afterlife, we likewise appeal to the Enemy's offspring with an appetizing form of heavenly materialism.

The Angry Deity

We know all anger, disgust, and disappointment was thrust on the One at the moment of the Work. We also know the Enemy would no more punish his children than a loving human father would beat a baby. What is intriguing, however, is that many patients are quick to attribute to their deity characteristics and actions so heinous that any human father would be incarcerated for the same!

For thousands of years, humans rightly assumed the Enemy to be reactionary, especially in regard to their sins. Under the old way of the law, many saw him angered at their sins, turning away from them, and withdrawing his blessings. But in these last days, even after the Work was fully accomplished, some of these imbeciles still believe the Enemy fumes with anger and disgust over them because of their performance. And since they will always continue to struggle with some form of sin, it only logically follows that the Enemy should be *perpetually* disappointed with them.

In keeping with this error, we can brainwash them with a general sense of shame, which they latch on to with an acute feeling of deserving. Consequently, they feel neither empowered for a life of victory nor qualified for a life of intimacy with the One.

Pushing Punishment

How do we coax new converts into believing the Enemy is angry with them despite the seemingly obvious effects of the Work? One trusted method is to suggest that the Work did not encompass all punishment and that there is more to come when they do wrong. Ancient human superstitions and the innate belief in what they term "karma" (bad actions deserving a consequence of like kind) leave some of their younger ones in particular open to this deception.

Vigorous assessment of an individual patient reveals when to suspend your efforts and when to strike. If the opportunity to introduce an angry or disappointed deity becomes available, take advantage swiftly and decisively. Concentrate on the goal and heap the shame. The distance between the Enemy and the patient himself will be perceived to increase. All the while, he is committing more and more sins, and his sin tabulations and confessions fall woefully short. Thus, he settles into a more permanent state of feeling distant from a deity who is continually irritated with him. Once he imagines the Enemy in this light, he grows discouraged, perhaps even depressed.

Over the centuries, we have observed that those given to isolation and other means of "purifying" themselves go so far as to engage in a self-scourging—a pure joy to witness! But whether it is physical, mental, or emotional pain that a patient inflicts upon himself is not important, as long as his view of the Work remains warped. He must be so consumed with his efforts to ward off the Enemy's disgust that he is completely blinded to the obvious—that the Enemy remembers his sins no more.

Do not let a patient comprehend the Work as the end of all punishment. Train him to anticipate some form, any form, of lesser but ongoing punishment rendered by the Enemy. If this is what he comes to expect, he will even begin to interpret life's tragic events as castigation from the Enemy. He will picture the Enemy hurling turmoil his way, whether it is poverty, sickness, or even the death of those around him. As he correlates these earthly circumstances with his recent performance, the Enemy's face is disfigured, and we blind the patient to the Blood.

6

000|0|11+/00001000101110090111u/100010./10/0/01011/1000110100000+011|01000|0111000001110/100010.1110u/0011/000011-101000000

Steal Celebration

We have already detailed how to secure various footholds when it comes to forgiveness. By now you have gained new insight into how to feed a patient the lie that he either suffers forms of punishment now or will one day undergo an impending judgment for his many sins. However, there is another nuance to our forgiveness-related efforts that we have yet to address.

Given that we so easily prey upon their weakness of conscience, we can convince the moronic mortals to accept the notion that the Enemy cannot use them in any way, as he is utterly horrified by the quantity or size of their sins. Our quiet infiltration of their thoughts leads them to believe they are washed up, unqualified for relationship or service.

After the barrage of condemnation we pile upon them, they easily miss the fact that the Book itself was written by murderers. The very patriarchs of their faith—Moses who killed in anger, David who killed for lust, and Paul who once killed their own kind—committed these lovely acts but then went on to serve the Enemy mightily. Nevertheless, we find that some patients readily persist in their belief that through their own personal failings, they disqualify themselves for service. They are impressed with the size of their sins rather than inspired by the wonder of the Work.

They cannot seem to fathom that by the Blood, the One has qualified them once and forever as ministers of his new way. Whether a sin was committed before or after their conversion makes no difference to him, as the Work has removed all record of it. Even the Ghost is tireless in his love affair with them. When we think of it all, our bile churns and we gag on our vomit.

Robbing Their Ritual

Of course, it is always our solemn duty to accuse them day and night, but their ceremonial meal is a time when we find them particularly vulnerable. Yes, even the celebration of their sacred supper offers opportunity to induce guilt and spoil the occasion. You simply pervert the purpose of the event in their minds such that they believe it is only to be celebrated by those who have first gone through an introspective purification ritual. Then you suck away their hope of enjoyment through a combination of attacks on multiple fronts.

Passages from the Book can be twisted to aid our cause. For example, we find that the phrase "let a man examine himself" affords us nearly limitless possibilities. We know, having been present in Corinth ourselves, that this examination refers to a church of long ago engaging in gluttony and drunkenness during the meal itself, and they were instructed to reform their practices. But this examination passage outside of its historical context can be used to incite all manner of self-accusation in patients today. As we whisper in their ears the need for examination, they inspect themselves week after week and month after month, wondering if they even qualify for the meal they are supposed to heartily partake of and rejoice over. In this way, we hold the Work under wraps. We disguise the meal as a ritual about *them*, not about the One. Then the game is ours, and *we* celebrate.

Even some of their leaders may assist you here. Do your utmost to convince those in management roles that a cleansing ritual of sorts is needed to purge the congregation before they celebrate the Body and the Blood. In some situations, we've encouraged the gullible clowns to darken the room, play ominous music, and carry their followers through an examination of all recent sins in order to qualify for the meal. We find that even some pleading, begging, and wailing in shame ensues.

Should this occur, you can be certain that a patient does not recognize the celebration for what it truly is. He has failed to acknowledge the sufficiency of the Work to qualify him for immediate celebration. Rather than inspecting the Work of the One, the patient inspects himself. Rather than analyzing the Blood, he analyzes his own recent track record. He looks to his sins, not his Savior. What was to be a feast of celebration becomes a feast of condemnation.

Your heart will leap at this delightful display signifying a job well done.

Spotlighting Sin Management

The uninformed deceiver might wonder, "As we guide them to examine and pore over their sins, will this not actually lead them to sin less in the long run?" This is a common misconception that we should address. It is true that the aforementioned stratagems designed to obscure forgiveness will incite a guilty conscience and imply that "sin management" is their goal. So at first glance, this may not seem the focus we should invoke in them. After all, is it not our objective to spur the Enemy's offspring to engage in *more* sin rather than "manage" it?

Allow us to explain. It all boils down to spotlighting something, anything, for them to fixate on such that they neglect the Life that inspires them to truly live. A seemingly spiritual focus is a much easier sell than one that is more obviously intended to lead them astray. So we make sin avoidance the message they receive. We can certainly afford for them to avoid the most overt of sinful actions if in doing so they obsess over sin management. As they seek to attain the sin-free standard, they set their minds on sin avoidance rather than walking by the Ghost. Hence they do reject certain sinful behaviors but continue in more subtle sins of another sort—entirely neglecting the expression of Life.

Essentially, they learn to fight overt forms of sin in their own strength in their needless attempts to remain cleansed and qualified. In an ironic twist, this only propels them to set their minds on a different kind of sin: self-improvement. They unwittingly place themselves under a form of law and only excite human effort. Therefore, sin is aroused, not stifled. Admittedly, it may be a different flavor of sin than the traditional tempter seeks to induce, but it is sin nonetheless and thus achieves our desired effect. Self-reliance and the corresponding pride are wonderful sins to foster in the unsuspecting fools, as these tend to endure for longer spans of time than any of the less socially acceptable sins.

dragon principle 2

7

00010111+/0000100010111000011101100010./1000/0101110001101000000111101000101110000111010001110110.1110001011100011-101000000

Kill Contentment

To kill a patient's contentment, offer him the faint suspicion that he deserves more happiness. Work up such a feeling of discontent in him that you lure him into continually seeking a change of circumstances. Then he will overlook the enduring joy that springs from celebrating the Work.

Given their dull, untrained senses, some patients perceive little more than the physical world around them. They naturally wander about, seeking to grab hold of what happiness they might find. If they conclude they have garnered less than their peers, they are well on their way toward desiring even more. Exactly what flavor of "more" we might goad them to crave varies from one patient to the next. Here we outline some general trends.

The Health Distraction

Some who suffer from physical ailments can be persuaded that the "more" they require is physical healing. The right strategy here is to introduce the idea that they have an Enemy-given right to be free from all illness and infirmity. As is often the case, some passages from the Book can be convoluted to reinforce the "promise" of guaranteed physical health.

We know that in adopting this view, they will presume more rights for themselves than did the One himself, who emptied himself of all rights and abandoned all but the dependent life, then suffered and died. But when it comes to rights and privileges, some patients believe they *deserve* to be treated more "fairly" than him! In his name they believe and teach that freedom from all physical ills is their earthly birthright. Despite one of their own apostles prescribing wine, not more faith, for frequent stomach ailments, this vein of deception still finds significant traction among them.

Once they are immersed in this line of thinking, we can subdue them in a constant state of disappointment. As they continue to confront physical challenges like all others on the planet, despite exercising belief and making "claims" to the contrary, they only grow more bewildered. Trapped in the quagmire of trying to generate more faith, they redouble their efforts rather than realizing that the *focus* of their faith is where they err. They lose confidence as we drag them into our pit of unrealistic expectation under the guise of the Enemy's "promises."

The Wealth Distraction

Efforts to stir discontent should not center on physical wellness alone. May it never be! Here we again call your attention to the historical, worldwide appeal of material wealth.

Yes, even though their Book speaks of being content with food and clothing, some patients are still susceptible to the ludicrous notion that the Work somehow bestows a promise of earthly fortune.

Of course, the Book contains admonitions warning against this very mindset. Their sacred writings disclose that affection for money brings on all manner of evil. The Book even notes that only men of depraved mind will purport that godliness is a means to financial gain. Still, many among them are willing, even eager, to succumb to that very depravity. Naturally, we stand ready to assist them down the alluring path.

Massage their fleshly egos. Appeal to the lust of the eyes, encouraging them that they need, deserve, and should claim material wealth in the Name. They easily equate correlation with causation. So if you bamboozle a few wealthy patients into supposing their faith in "claiming wealth" has steered them toward financial gain, they will turn and promise the masses the same if they too will only believe.

When the majority fail at the mental exercise of claiming wealth, they will burn with frustration. Whether a given patient ends up materially wealthy or poor makes no difference. Either way, we channel his affections away from his true birthright. As with Esau of long ago, we coerce him to exchange enjoyment of the Life he already possesses for a hope no more enduring than a bowl of soup.

On Trouble and Trials

Not all patients are inclined to believe they have a divine guarantee of health or wealth on earth. Many are too discerning for such a scheme. In such cases, you may discover that a third deception is viable: the idea that the Enemy will not allow them to experience more than they can withstand. Of course, to erroneously conclude this, they misunderstand one Scripture and neglect another. But once the hope of smooth sailing is set, when circumstances of their world hit, they are confused by their inability to cope. So they question themselves and the Enemy, asking, "How could this be happening to me when I have put full trust in him to keep me from it?"

Bewildered, they wonder where is the One in whom they believed for safe passage without overwhelming obstacles and difficulty. With unrealistic expectations in place, they do not even look for his comfort or counsel in the midst of turmoil. Instead they only look for the magic words or mental exercise that will somehow deliver them from the circumstances themselves. When this does not happen for them in any timely fashion, we bind them in a state of confusion about the nature of the Enemy's love.

Of course, this gives rise to doubt about the validity of the Work itself. Some will ask what good the Work is at all if it does not remove their troubles. A secondary effect is that those who claim to believe away their troubles are forced to don a mask of emotional affluence when trials hit, so as not to be perceived as spiritual weaklings unable to claim the very promises they promote.

Keep them wondering, and thereby defend the occupied stronghold of "failed promises." If you are not careful, they will piece together the truth and discover they have no spiritual right to the cushy circumstances they set their faith on. If they surrender these rights and submit to the Life alone as their one solid hope, they will see how to give thanks in the midst of any circumstance. Territory once delivered to the Enemy is nearly impossible to regain.

Conclusion

Whether we persuade patients to fixate on health, or wealth, or the comfort of changed circumstances makes no difference. In each case, they are blinded to the One who relinquished his rights, and they cannot even imagine that taking on the same mindset is the route to freedom. Instead, they invest in a message opposed to the Work itself and are grounded in our glorious alternative.

When circumstances do not align with their "rights," many patients will resort to a quantity of prayers or to very bossy prayers, believing they should boldly claim promises or convince the Enemy through a volume of petitions. This builds on the ancient pagan paradigm that gods are easily distracted and need reminders in order to be appeased and pay attention to their worshipers. Whenever possible, it is wise to draw upon natural assumptions like these, as the average patient is predisposed toward them already. It only makes the inevitable disappointment that much sweeter to observe.

8

00010111+/00001000101110000110/100010./18/0/0101 1/100011010000+011101000101110000110/100010..111000101110000011-101000000

Kill Focus

In this chapter we unlock winning concepts to steal away a patient's time, achieving a significant negative effect on his long-term development. Using refined targeting, it is possible to busy a patient and send him off like a rat scurrying through an endless maze. But as fun as this may sound, it is always vital that you move based on accurate intelligence to ensure efficacy. Having synthesized the current data in our archives, we outline for you here two of the best approaches to thieving away a patient's time to the delight of Our Father Below.

The Enemy's Will

Recall that stealthy, unobtrusive methods work best, as we continue to go undetected. Once you set a given belief system in motion, it can perpetuate itself among them apart from any direct intervention. One such system involves the idea of finding and seeking to remain in the Enemy's "will." Here their human tendencies toward superstition serve as fuel easily lit by just a few choice measures.

We begin with some background information. The Book states nothing about trying to "find" his will as if it were yet undiscovered. Instead it reveals his will in a rather straightforward fashion. The Enemy's will is this: to present the Message to those from every nation; to renew his children's minds such that they bear fruit; and to instill in them a boldness to talk openly with him. In short, the Enemy's will is the One, expressed in them and through them.

Nevertheless, most do not realize how plainly the Enemy has spoken concerning his will. So we can anthropomorphize him, casting him as a human parent with rigid views of what his offspring should do to remain in his ever elusive will. In turn, they will see themselves as diviners needing to deduce the myriad avenues they must choose to continue in right standing. You will even induct their teachers into this way of thought. Then not only can you send patients off on this fruitless endeavor, but their own leaders will assist you, giving their followers a "formula" for finding the Enemy's will and then remaining in it.

This propels them to seek subtle signals they feel will lead to safe choices, free of difficulty. Some will sit paralyzed, waiting to hear which house, which spouse, which job, or which car is right for them. When things go smoothly with their choices, they will praise the Enemy. But when "right" choices end in difficulty or even disaster, we exploit their naïveté, burning into their minds overpowering questions about the Enemy: *Where is he now? How could he direct me to this decision only to have the outcome be so tragic?*

Some will assume they merely miscalculated in their discerning of divine signals. Others will doubt their own level of tenacity in seeking his will. Maybe they didn't try hard enough; maybe they didn't seek long enough; or maybe they didn't listen well enough. Perhaps they could not hear properly because their lives are inundated with sin. This will drive some to seek out every so-called sin blockage, attempting to confess themselves into a cleansed state where they can finally perceive the Enemy's will. These tend to be the neurotic ones, but even if you bring the masses only a bit closer to this anxiety, you have done well.

This framework inevitably leads to all manner of self-analysis and results in various flavors of fear: fear they might, in ignorance, make a poor decision that places them outside his will forever; or even fear that they've *already* made some deliberate choice that cast them outside his will, perhaps even permanently.

The underlying assumption motivating them is that if they can locate the "perfect will" of the Enemy and stay in it, they will continue to be right with him, and their circumstances will be pleasant. Here they unknowingly seek a form of *righteousness!* Trying to get right and stay right with the Enemy by making various choices is a works righteousness that many of them would publicly denounce. Still, the fools do not seem to notice the glaring error in their personal belief system. And their leaders only feed the psychosis when they imply that the Enemy heartily approves of their never-ending quest for his will in *everything*.

Again, in all of this they neglect the Enemy's straightforward desire for them—that they arise each day and present their bodies to him, give thanks in all things, and bear his fruit in an atmosphere of freedom. One of their own well-known teachers once instructed them to simply love the Enemy and then live as they please. Still, most patients fail to see that the Enemy's will is the Ghost himself radiated in and through their unique personalities, no matter what heart-led choices they might make. They do not perceive the liberty of the Life. So at whatever cost, do not let them discover it!

Divining the Future

While some are obsessed with being situated in the Enemy's will, others are more apt to concern themselves with endless calculations and speculations about the future. This distraction also stems from a most basic human desire—to know what tomorrow will bring.

Carefully ascertain whether a patient might be susceptible to this sort of diversion, and if you deem him a good candidate, then set him in motion to use the Book much like a crystal ball. This will sidetrack him in his reading of the Book, diverting attention away from what is of utmost importance—the meaning of the Work.

We know that true prophecy in this present age involves exhortation, consolation, and edification by speaking truth about the Work. But their understanding of prophecy has been so distorted that many believe it to be fortune- or future-telling. It takes only a little skill on our part to further this mindset, as they easily forget there is no adding to or taking away from prophecies already put forth in the Book.

The most alluring prediction of all involves the return of the One. To this day I am refreshingly amazed at the number of patients swayed into believing they can foresee his return, even calculate it with inventive mathematics. Despite the One himself affirming that no one can know such things and that he will enter like a thief in the night, some essentially suppose they can outwit the Enemy, unveiling his planned return. In their arrogance, some narrow it to a day or hour when they cannot even know the epoch.

As we incite these prophecies and arouse the egos of those who assert them, we achieve a great deal in undermining the faith. These fortune-tellers are easily inflated by their own importance, some even equating themselves with prophets of old. Their confident pronouncements, even when unverifiable or wrong, attract weak-minded vermin in droves. And after witnessing failed predictions made by a "prophet" once respected, who wouldn't begin to doubt them as mouthpieces of any truth at all? Patients lose trust in the charlatans who misled them, and a glorious shadow of doubt is cast over the whole message of Life.

9

0001011+/0001000101100001110/10001011010011010100000+011101000101110000111101000101110000011101010111000011-101000000

Kill Resources

1t can be dispiriting for any novice tempter to encounter a public reading of the Book. For example, sometimes we are forced to stand by and hear that the Enemy's divine power has granted the cretins everything they need for life and godliness. Or perhaps, through the Book, we might hear the Enemy assuring them that he will meet all their needs. Passages like these are sufficient to send any sincere, eager agent into a flaming tailspin.

But do not despair. It is relatively simple (once you get the hang of it) to sow seeds of doubt in a patient's mind concerning the reliability of those very promises. The aforementioned truths seem so grandiose, so all-encompassing, that it is only natural for the clodpates to caveat them, thinking of ways they do not or cannot apply. We merely aid the process by interposing with the right thought at the right time. Then we stand back and watch as they walk down the path of unbelief we paved for them.

Do not permit them to be satisfied. Instead, bring them into such a state of mind that they furiously seek to obtain more. If we can foster an insatiable sense that they need more than they currently possess, they will not pause long enough to realize they have already been given everything they need through the presence of the One within them.

Good reconnaissance always stacks the odds in your favor, so learn everything you can about a particular patient. Over the centuries, we have collected data from hosts of field operatives. Our empirical studies reveal that two deceptions in particular consistently bring about beneficial effects: (1) the belief that they need *more faith*, and (2) the belief that they need *more love* for the Enemy and their fellow humans.

Chasing Faith

First, we seek to make patients into faith chasers. How? Through emotion, we change perception. We produce within them a sense of lack, and then we assault their minds with the accusation that they need more faith. Through simultaneous application of multiple pressures, we cause them to falsely perceive a deficit.

If we fix in their minds the idea that they have insufficient faith to "claim" the Enemy's goodness in whatever form it might take, then what benefit will he be to them? So we feed their self-deception that they need more faith, and they in turn come to value (even obsess over) the *size* of their faith rather than the *object* of their faith. Yes, despite their occasional rant about how faith the size of a mustard seed is sufficient, we still persuade the egomaniacs that faith is what they conjure up, more and more, until their sizable faith makes something happen. Then we have them well in hand.

Make sure they do not recognize that they now live by a measure of faith already apportioned to them through the One. That sort of revelation is dangerous and should be swiftly altered. Instead, make them attend to a whirlwind of questions: *Do I have enough faith? Is my faith big enough? How can I get more faith?* Employing first person singular pronouns (*I, me, my*) while posing as their conscience, *you* are the one asking the questions and therefore maintain the upper hand. They cry out, begging for more faith, and look for any evidence of their answered cry.

We have seen this approach yield two main benefits for our operation. First, they center on themselves and their own faithfulness rather than the trustworthy character of the faithful One. Second, from this new angle we once again have them pleading for spiritual riches they already possess through the Ghost.

Chasing Love

When we find patients unmoved by accusations against their faith, we turn their attention toward needing *more love*.

Love is wonderfully nebulous, as it cannot actually be quantified. So if they seek to love the Enemy more, failure is guaranteed from the outset. They will never attain to a standard of outwardly loving the Enemy in a measurable way commensurate with what he deserves. Consequently, as they project the human notion of entitlement on him, they will never feel he is satisfied with the quantity of love they have for him. Envisioning either his broken heart of disappointment or his scowl of disapproval, they will wallow in disgust at themselves. Watching this transpire is a most pleasing form of entertainment.

Of course, it is the Enemy who loved them first, and they are only designed to absorb and respond to that love. But once we have them measuring their love and condemning themselves for not loving him more, they are blinded to this divine order. So they recommit themselves to loving him more and all the while lose sight of the catalyst—*his radical, undying love for them.*

Keep them from grasping the depths of his love. Should the eyes of their hearts be opened, patients may well up with gratitude and a corresponding love for both the Enemy and others. If those outside the Body take note of this, they might inquire as to the hope within these otherwise boring creatures. So our objective is to keep the Enemy's love for them out of their minds altogether. Provoking them to guilt about their lack of love for him and then steering them to muster up more love helps us achieve this goal.

Conclusion

Always keep them searching for *more*. Yes, they already have everything they need for life and godliness. Yes, they have already been blessed with every spiritual blessing in the One. But we must take captive any thoughts of that sort and keep them in a haze of doubt, wondering, *How can I get more faith? How can I get more love? Don't I need more of these before I can truly begin living from the Life?*

If they knew the riches of the Life they possess, they would stop seeking and start living. But if we do our job well, they will squander the opportunity to give thanks for the faith and love right under their noses.

So keep them perpetually searching. Fix their eyes on a *future* hope of more. They won't even begin to imagine that a full infusion of the Life has already occurred and that they are complete. They won't realize they have all the faith and love they ever need. They won't see that their hope is *now*.

10

0001011+/0001001011100001110/100010./10/0/0101/1000110100000+0111010001011100001110/100010. 1110001011100001110100000

Kill Life

It is nearly impossible to conceal the fact that salvation involves getting sins forgiven. There simply are no patients unaware, at least to some degree, of that truth. But this is not the most important aspect of their salvation. The very essence of salvation itself is not forgiveness but receiving the Life through the indwelling of the Sacred Ghost.

If they understand forgiveness alone to be the whole Message, the deluded simpletons will live impotent lives, waiting for a hope that is to come.

If they buy into a partial truth—that the One died to forgive them, enabling safe passage to heaven someday—then we have much to work with. But if they should perceive the second half of the Work—that the One was raised to give his own resurrection life to them—they will connect with the dynamic empowerment the early church once knew.

We cannot allow them to see the Life.

Winning the War

We do sympathize with your fears about entering into battles that concern the Ghost himself. It is justifiable that even the bravest and most aggressive among us hesitate when it comes to this sort of conflict. After all, no tactic, not even the most devious and well-executed attack, succeeds against the Ghost himself. He is impervious to our most effective stratagems. We must always be realistic about what is possible and what is impossible, as there are some battles we are guaranteed to lose.

Nevertheless, remember that our goal is not to win every battle but to win the war. Being able to distinguish the one from the other is crucial to our long-term success. So despite the fact that he who is in them is greater than all of us combined, we still have one overwhelming advantage against the obtuse half-wits: many simply do not know what it means to possess the Life. They are not acquainted with the power and resources within them. Hence, our best strategy is to occlude the Life from them, so their minds do not perceive his presence. This is effectively accomplished by means of distraction.

The Enemy as Priority

Of all our strategies to hide the Life, nothing succeeds more frequently than having patients attempt to "put the Enemy first." At first glance, this might appear to be counter to our overall mission, but here you will learn why this is indeed not the case. (Note that this strategy is so effective with them for the same reason that *you* may doubt our use of it—putting the Enemy first seems so honorable and good!)

Of course, because of the Work, the One is now their very Life, as he has deposited his essence within their human spirits. Just beneath their skin and bones is the dwelling place of the Ghost himself. They are sacred little temples. But if we can divert their minds into regarding the Enemy as nothing more than a "priority" competing with their jobs, their families, and their free time, then he is not *Life itself* to them in the midst of *every* priority. He is pigeonholed into a tiny corner of their lives; he becomes an activity, one obligation among many.

Just as the mythological Greek king Sisyphus was condemned to perpetually push a boulder uphill, only to watch it roll back down again, we find these shortsighted peons who spend their time trying to put the Enemy "first" inevitably perceive him as sliding back down their list of priorities in a matter of days. In trying to keep him at the top of their agenda, they lose sight of the One as Life. They conceive of him as nothing more than an important commitment. (In observing their New Year's resolutions alone, we witness what happens to their "important" commitments!)

To measure their success in giving the One the proper place he deserves, patients generally direct their attention to church or religious activity. They suppose that the more time they spend with these affairs, the more they must be giving the Enemy priority. The reality is that the busier they are performing what they perceive as the only "spiritual" activities, the less likely they will be to recognize the divine Life that is fused to theirs, without interruption. They will fail to rest in the ever-present Life designed to animate *every* aspect of their lives.

Spiritual and Secular

Because a patient's entire life is now immersed in the One, everything he does can be a spiritual act of worship. However, most patients seem slow to believe their situation to be so good. Instead, they regard some actions as holy and others as sinful, and they even hold to the existence of a third category of "neutral" acts. This third type, in their eyes, comprises the majority of their existence. Given the helpfulness of this framework to us, the informed deceiver watches patients carefully to ensure they maintain this view. We cannot permit them to contemplate the idea that everything they do can be set apart, distinguished, even heavenly.

Help them set up standards by which to judge the relative spiritual importance of their actions. Aid them in dividing their activities into a "spiritual" category, a "sinful" category, and a nearly all-encompassing "neutral" category. For most, their weekly meetings, studies, services, and nonprofit projects will belong to the spiritual category. But many will inevitably see the remainder of their lives as involving mundane, everyday matters that are of little or no relevance to the One. So keep them looking to *the nature of the activity itself* rather than *the One motivating them* to determine an activity's importance or worth. As they adopt this perspective, they will not give serious consideration to the radical notion that every aspect of their lives can be a divine expression of the Ghost.

His Presence in Places

To further a view of the Ghost's *conditional* presence, sell them on the idea that he visits or dwells in the physical places they worship instead of being housed literally within them. Passages in the Book describing the old way of the law will assist in promoting this view.

Have them imagine the Ghost as swooping down to fill their worship venues with his presence. If we fill their minds with the idea that his presence is reliant on their buildings, their music, and their reading of the Book, they will inevitably conclude he is not very present the remainder of the time. They will settle for less, and we will accomplish more.

All of this will undoubtedly lead them to hunt for new experiences, or "revival," each time they feel a prolonged emotional drag. They will look for spiritual renewal of his presence through events that they expect him to "attend." Over and over, they will seek a fresh anointing of the Ghost and pursue more power for upright living.

Their leaders can be used to repeatedly challenge them to hunger for more, never settling or being satisfied with the supposed "little" they currently possess of the One. This despite the One himself telling them they would hunger no more.

So we work alongside these leaders, convincing their masses that they are in need of more of the Ghost. Followers will assume they are not yet complete. They will not even imagine that they can awake every day and labor according to his power and intimate presence already at work within them.

Finally, a thorough attack will encompass their prayer life. Push them to pray for more of the Ghost, a second and third portion. In all their supplications, let them forget that the Enemy poured out his love into their hearts through the Sacred Ghost and permanently equipped them with himself. As they open the door to the sales pitch of his conditional presence, they shut out an authentic revelation of the Life already theirs.

All of Him, None of Them

While patients plead and beg for more of the Sacred Ghost, we do well to cultivate an underlying sense that they are not truly compatible with his holiness. Work to promote the idea that they need to remove themselves from the spiritual equation altogether. Popular catchphrases such as "all of him and none of me" and "let go, let God" can be helpful to our cause. With sufficient repetition, some converts elevate these as ideas on par with the Book itself.

Herein we obscure their union with the One and subtly pit patients against him without them even being cognizant of it. We invoke in them a belief system that presumes they are part of the problem rather than the solution. Their world religions abound with followers seeking to "empty" themselves in order to possess more of whatever deity or spirit they might imagine. Because so many are predisposed toward self-loathing, we find our advances are easily accepted.

In conclusion, we must not allow patients to envision themselves as co-laborers, joined with the One.

Instead we present them with the image of being a hollow tube that from time to time is infused by the Ghost for acts of service. We can afford for them to adopt this view. But the permanent fusion of their human spirit together with his? This revelation must be thwarted by whatever means possible.

11

00010111+/00001000101110000111010001000100101011100011010000+011101001101100011010001011000101110000811-101000000

Kill Holiness

Amazingly, humans seem to have no issue with mild or even major discrepancies between what the Enemy says about them and what they feel is true in their own experience. Many of these stupid saints prefer to view their spiritual condition through a lens of their own natural senses, lending more authority to these than to the Book itself, whenever the two appear to contradict. This phenomenon of favoring their own mental perceptions is particularly evident when it comes to their identity. While the Book itself calls them "holy ones" dozens of times, you can still ensure they never personalize the identity, taking it to heart. How do you prevent this? Here we suggest two ways.

Reducing Sainthood

First, suggest to them that it is only proper to think of masses of converts as "saints." Make certain they remain uneasy about the notion that they *individually* are literally and actually a holy saint. Don't let them shake the sinner label; it is a tool we cannot lose.

Even if you find patients adopting the "saint" label, our records indicate we can still convince them of a twofold identity. They will regard themselves as simultaneously sinner and saint, and many will believe it is more humble and educated to do so. Of course, we know that true humility means seeing themselves in the same way the Enemy does, no more and no less. We convince them, though, that for them to take on his view in any real, tangible sense is arrogance in its most despicable and heretical form.

Tell them their hearts are desperately wicked and it is only godly honesty to admit it. They should believe it is humble and accurate to call themselves "chief of sinners" just as our vile nemesis Paul once did. In adopting Paul's statement for themselves, they will fail to realize he was merely describing his *former* life as a persecutor of the Body.

If we convince patients they are sinners by nature, dirty at their core, they will not live like holy offspring of the Enemy. They will don their former label of sinner, and this inevitably carries all kinds of pleasant consequences for us. After all, what is the most natural thing for a sinner to do? Sin, of course! So make them believe they *want* to sin. Tell them that their sworn duty is to resist their *own* desire to sin. This will only excite the flesh and put human effort into motion. It will also subtly suggest to them that their new life in the One is essentially an invitation to be fake as they combat their own nature, attempting to act differently than the sin-loving hypocrites they really are!

We find that many of their hymns and songs can be used to bolster the case against them. If the leader who selects their songs lacks the discernment to distinguish between the old life and the redeemed one, he inevitably tutors his followers in the very error we seek to perpetuate. Through these suggestive tunes, children of the Enemy intuit that they are nothing more than dirty worms hoping for the day when they will finally be changed into beautiful butterflies. They believe they are impure and imperfect, needing to be cleansed again and again. They think they are in need of a new heart and a right spirit nearly every week! With these suppositions implanted, they do not see the beauty the One has already bestowed upon them. In neglecting the glory given, royal priests wander about like the poorest of peasants.

Do not allow them to grasp the lofty post to which they have been appointed. We cannot have them celebrate with any measure of real joy. Their joy is an infectious disease that will spread among them and even waft toward heaven as a fragrant aroma to their King. To us, it is a putrid stench.

Halfway Holy

The second way to carry out this identity theft among them is to cloud their concept of holiness. We know children of the Enemy are as holy and set apart for him as they will ever be. While their attitudes and actions are being renewed, they cannot possibly set *themselves* apart any further. Through the Work, they were made perfectly holy, once and for all. They have already become people of his possession, reserved for him. No action of their own could ever make this more true, and any attempt to do so is a waste of time and effort. So what should our goal be other than to have them waste time and effort as they seek to make themselves *more* holy?

The first step is to establish a solid basis for their continuing efforts. We need to persuade them they are becoming holy progressively as they cleanse and devote themselves more fully. In all of this, our hope is that they will always equate who they are (their identity) with what they do (their performance).

The amateur deceiver might think the Book would only hurt our cause here, but this situation is another exception to the rule. It can indeed be helpful to recall a number of passages related to the holiness of their *actions*. These can be easily distorted such that they buy into a progressive personal holiness. Some will even tremble at what state of holiness they might be in when they meet the Enemy face-to-face.

It is imperative to suggest creative and tangible ways these fabulously ignorant fools can make themselves more holy. Recall that most humans live only from an awareness of the *physical* world around them. Therefore, even after their new birth, they naturally root their ideas about progressive holiness in what can be seen. Some focus on clothing, wearing long flowing robes that visually set them apart from the population. Others geographically remove themselves from the rest of the population, building compounds that protect them from outside influences and preserve their supposed holiness. Finally, others believe themselves to be set apart by their activity—whether it be their religious schooling, church activities, or other types of "holy" living. These include abstaining from marriage, avoiding a particular food or drink, or celebrating certain religious holy days while others do not. All of these give patients the sense that they have come out from among the masses and are made holy (set apart) through external acts.

The avenue to holiness a given patient pursues matters little to us. The only thing of importance is that he invests in any of these to affect his progressive "level" of personal holiness. Consequently, he will fail to see that he is indwelt by the Sacred Ghost himself, and since the Ghost is holy, the patient *must* already be entirely holy himself at the very core of his being. Yet even when the naïve wretches refer to themselves as the Ghost's temple, they do somehow miss the point. We find them quite inclined to picture themselves as a temple containing numerous filthy rooms awaiting a future cleaning.

In sum, we delight in observing their fruitless attempts to attain a holiness already given to them. Even when one of their own kind hints at the idea that they are holy, they immediately resort to the fact that it was only a gift. And from our vantage point, it seems to be a gift they refuse to truly own.

12

00010111+/00001000101110000011l0/100010../10/0/010l1/10001101000+011101000l0111000011l0/100010.1110001011l000011-10l000000

Kill Righteousness

 ou might not think it possible to conceal a patient's own death from him, but let us assure
you—you have much to learn. Many patients see
eternal life as merely their life made better or their
life made longer. When they consider the Work,
they think only of the One himself. They do not
readily see themselves as *included in* the Work, dying
together with him and beginning an entirely new and
altogether different life united with him.

Counterfeit Crucifixion

While their expression "born again" has become popular in some circles, it has largely lost its intended meaning. Empty repetition has served as our ally here, and familiarity has even bred contempt. They have grown so callous to the term that it is now little more than a political or social label, and many outsiders even abhor the term. This was not our doing; it simply fell in our laps. But we could not have been more pleased when it did. (Sometimes you just get lucky, you know.)

Now, we know their old selves were once slaves to our domain. But through their death in the One, they were liberated from our control. Nevertheless, many of their kind do not even realize this, so we work to conceal their inner transformation. How do we accomplish this? Accuse them with their current experience, demonstrating how counterfeit the notion of being "new" must actually be. Whisper to them that if they *feel* sinful and weakened by sin's power, then they certainly must be sinful at the core. Urge them to believe that to betray their feelings would be hypocrisy. Smuggle in the idea that passages from the Book concerning their inner transformation must only refer to the Enemy's "view" of them, an identity not actualized until they finally receive glorified bodies from above.

Their crucifixion with the One must go unde- tected. If many of them realize it as a literal and actual death and rebirth at the core of their being, it could be devastating to our cause. But if any patient should get wind of his new birth and its true implications, we can nip that sort of thinking in the bud, containing the damage. We simply cast him as a fanatic who has twisted a symbolic truth into something literal. This works like a charm, as most patients quickly back off and give way to the scholars around them who know just how to properly "categorize" certain truths. In this way, we infuse significant uncertainty into the situation, and as a result, they become enmeshed in endless speculations about whether a truth is sym- bolic or real, positional or actual. Their most learned types explain away the reality of their death in the One with fine-sounding rhetoric, and any "simplistic" view of truth never sees the light of day.

Hide the Other Half

Remember that their death in the One is only half the story. Let them do anything except grasp the second half of the Work—the resurrection. If you find part of the truth has been carried out into the light, there is still one possible measure to occlude the whole.

Many appear content to believe the resurrection occurred merely for the Enemy to prove his power over death. But it is the *personal* effects of the resurrection in their lives that are hazardous to us. We cannot allow its impact to be known.

So let them say, "I died with him." Let them declare themselves to be dead to sin. Let them serve as spiritual corpses, lifeless servants of their King. Just don't permit them to see themselves as *alive*, joined to the Ghost, and compatible with the Life itself. We cannot afford for them to know the Message carries a present and powerful reality. If they give the resurrection the credence it deserves, then *all* hope is lost.

Rethinking Righteousness

For humans, righteousness is the ultimate prize. It is in essence the goal nearly all of them seek, regardless of which world religion they ascribe to. Given how highly they value righteousness, it might seem that diverting a patient's attention away from the gift of righteousness in the One would be impossible. After all, how could we distract them from something so greatly treasured? But the reality is that with a bit of simple wordplay and a bait-and-switch technique, we keep their righteousness under wraps.

How is this carried out? First, we remind you to always locate their vulnerabilities. Surely, even your limited encounters with patients have unveiled their proclivity to regard spiritual truth as nearly irrelevant to their present life. Given that fact, just imagine what they might be willing to conclude about their righteousness.

For example, we find them easily persuaded that the Enemy merely views them "as if" they are righteous while they are not actually righteous in any real sense in the here and now. Alternatively, we find many of them willing to believe that they are *becoming* righteous progressively as they learn to behave in such a way. This is, of course, an earned righteousness, but for some reason they do not perceive it as such.

Now, we realize that all of this must seem quite absurd to you in view of the clarity contained within the Book. After all, it plainly reveals that they have become the very righteousness of the Enemy himself! Nevertheless, rest assured that we can and do help them reinterpret these kinds of ideas quite effectively.

We stealthily whisper to them that they possess a righteousness "of sorts." We tell them that it is how the Enemy views them from afar. Or we tell them that it is merely a promise of righteousness they will one day receive. Or we tell them that when the Enemy looks upon them, he sees the One *instead* of them (and if the Enemy were to actually see them, he would be mortified!).

Essentially, we tell them whatever we need to tell them, short of the truth. And with a bit of poking concerning their recent sins, this usually does the trick. When confronted with a subtle attack like this, it seems that believing in any literal, actual righteousness only feels like hypocrisy to them. They wonder, *How could I really be a righteous new creation if so much unrighteous thinking persistently billows through my mind?* Assuming they are the sole source of their thought life, that they are responsible as the origin of every thought therein, they altogether discredit the idea that righteousness has been imparted to them. And as with their holiness, they relegate their righteousness to a useless bin of "positional" truth.

Conclusion

We know that genuine humility for them is to look upon themselves just as the Enemy does, and in so doing they see *reality*. But with relative ease we encourage them to hold tightly to the false humility of being an "unrighteous sinner" with a "wicked heart." We do whatever we can to foster the perception that they are dirty and distant followers of a deity who barely tolerates them. They must view themselves as servants who fight against their very selves in the hope of attaining real righteousness at a future date. We cannot afford for them to see that their righteousness is real and that their righteousness is now. After all, what if they should end up living in that sort of quiet confidence? May it never be!

13

Kill Discernment

From day one, patients know they are involved in a spiritual war within them. But the nature of that conflict and the allies and opponents involved are not always so clear.

We use this to our advantage. We have witnessed that hordes of them interpret sinful temptations as originating from within themselves, and many even interpret our accusations of them as coming from the Ghost himself! So with a consistent cycle of temptation and accusation, we keep them in a state of confusion about who they are and which side they are really fighting on. If we can convince them that their nature—the spiritual center of their being—is still on our side, then we have them right where we want them. But if they realize they are joined to the One and that even their *own* nature is now opposed to us, they become infinitely harder to entice.

A House Divided

The One himself spoke of how a house divided cannot stand. We do well to take this to heart. A most useful tool—the flesh—can be used to project a false perception that they are indeed a house divided.

To uninformed patients, the flesh is perceived to be a part of their identity, a sinful nature within them. Holding this view, they act as if the Work has not yet been applied to them. They fail to recognize the flesh as a separate entity tempting them from outside their new, regenerated spirit. Instead, they see it as their old self or old nature fighting against their new self. Although already crucified and buried, their old self is perceived to have come storming out of the tomb to haunt them. In their minds, it coexists alongside the new creation. It is important to keep patients from learning any different.

The whole concept of living as "a house divided" sounds ridiculous to *us*, as we see clearly it is not the case. We know they are completely new at their core. We see it, but surprisingly they cannot. Without their resurrection eyes, humans are not adept at discerning spiritual entities. They walk only by faith, not by sight. They rely exclusively on what they are taught, either from the Book or, in many cases, from those apt to go with what they *feel* is true.

Their spiritual naïveté gives us plenty to work with as we attack at the doorway of their minds. They mistake one source of thoughts, the flesh, for another—the old self already crucified, buried, and gone. They conclude that the flesh is them, or at least "half" of them, and they live in the duality of a house divided.

Of course, they are in the One and free to reject thoughts of the flesh. But if they are not acquainted with this reality, they will act as slaves of the flesh, believing they actually desire to obey its cravings. They will perceive the flesh to be an evil half-identity left over from before their conversion. It will be to them an entity they somehow both love and detest.

And as they think in this way, so will they act—in utter double-mindedness.

So when they seek to explain their ongoing struggles with sin, the flesh masquerading as their old self serves as the perfect scapegoat. In this way, we convince them that they *want* to sin, that they *want* to disobey the Enemy, that their hearts *want* sin. Inundate them with this notion, not allowing them to arrive at any alternative interpretation of their thought lives. And if they have suffered persistently strong temptations in their recent history, our message of duality generally finds fertile ground. Humans are anxious to invoke any belief system that seems to explain their struggles, so if we hit them early and often, it is our doctrine of deception they will adopt.

Accusing Day and Night

This may sound like a sufficient measure to fatigue them, but there is more to consider here. Most converts are unaware that through our initial victory thousands of years ago, the power of sin has gained access to them through their earthly bodies. So when our sin parasite and the flesh work in tandem to deliver temptation, it is impossible for them not to sometimes feel as if they are both a "good me" and a "bad me." This split view of themselves—being half good and half evil—is a personhood readily accepted by many of them. Some welcome it with open arms, because it offers an intriguing theology that appears to reconcile their "new creation" passages with the daily temptations we launch within them.

Little do they know this very belief system submerges them in a wilderness of confusion. And once we secure in them this schizophrenic view, it is the easiest thing in the world to separate them from any real sense of righteousness and to spur them on to evil deeds. After all, how can they possibly resist us once they believe the sinful desires come directly from themselves? We have yet to encounter any human who can consistently deny what he believes is his own nature.

Furthermore, every time they try to do right, they feel they are acting *counter* to their real (sinful) identity. The icing on the cake is the one-two punch this affords us, as we can first present them with a sinful thought and then immediately accuse them of generating that thought! Posing as the Ghost himself, we express such disgust with their thought life that they in turn relegate themselves to a miserable experience, believing the Enemy is ashamed of their very existence. Long term, the most sincere of them are crushed under the weight of consternation, while others merely settle into the life that temptation offers and feel unqualified for anything different. This is the nature of our game, and whichever the outcome, our victory is imminent.

Tailored Temptation

If they do perceive the presence of sin and the flesh and realize their innate desire to turn from these, all is not lost. You can still work to *limit their concept of the flesh*.

If a patient is only aware of the overtly evil-looking flavors of flesh, you can still encourage him to build his identity around fleshly "goodness." And if he continues unaware of the self-improving flesh he employs, the kind that seeks to "perfect" its host, you can easily distract him from Ghost-led thoughts. He will take great pride in his education, his social status, his wealth, or even his virtue. In this way, you keep him well fed with fleshly satisfaction. Having begun by the Ghost, he will seek to better himself by fleshly effort, without even realizing it. Note that many of their leaders will not only condone but also promote this approach to "godliness"!

So let all temptations be suited to each individual. If a subject is apt to be low on himself, feed into that lowness, bringing him lower than ever. If another thinks himself to be something of repute according to the flesh, then cater to that pride and coax him to be more inflated than ever. The goal is to ensure the patients' slavery to anything that serves as distraction from the Life. As they feast on any fleshly identity we provide them, they perceive no way to rise above it and experience their birthright.

dragon principle 3

DESTROY

14

00010111+/00001000101110000111010000010. /10/0/0101 l/10001101000+011101000101110000111010/100010. 1110001011100011-10100900

Destroy Grace

hen it comes to winning against the Enemy's offspring, our approaches must suit individual circumstances. But in general, a large-scale approach to gain psychological dominance over them is to obscure the Work as the dividing line of human history. In many ways, we look back on the old way of the law with nostalgia, as its standards could never be satisfied. Being under its curse propelled even the most devout toward *more* sin. The power of sin has always been in the law, and the game just is not the same without it.

We know the Work rendered the old way obsolete and ushered in the new way we so rightly despise. So what can we accomplish in this discouraging new era? Thankfully, the ignorance of today's patients affords us a simple stratagem: don't let them come to know the liberty of the new way.

In short, hide the divide. Benumb their minds with the idea that they are under both ways at once. Induce them to squander their experience of the Life by smothering them with a balanced concoction of law and grace. Here you should become tutors of their own leadership. Train them to instruct followers that the Ghost has come to "help them obey" the old way. As they invite others to follow the law, we know, even as the Book itself proclaims, that sin will only increase among them. Once they place themselves under the curse of the law, they arouse the flesh to make attempts at "godly" obedience. The result will be the opposite of what they intend but precisely what we desire.

Concerning their reading of the Book, direct them to the old way as often as you can, flooding them with thoughts of obligation. By obscuring the dividing line of the Work, we sustain them in the unhappy marriage of old and new, and we steal away their freedom. Rather than seeing the Work as the end of the old way, teach them to accuse and then ostracize those who claim such things. Don't allow them to even suspect that living in that sort of liberty might be possible.

Inevitably, some will *insist* there is a great divide. So for those who seek to divide old from new, suggest that the divide occurred at the birth of the One, *not* at his death. This will bring significant confusion, as patients attempt to live uprightly via the same "be perfect" and "sell everything" teachings that the One employed to amplify the futility of the old way of works. And when they earnestly seek to live by *every* word he uttered, without regard for audience or context, we will hold them awake at night, pouring over them a bewildering despair. Their Father's face will grow disfigured, like that of a cruel dictator barking out impossible orders.

Notice that here we leverage their own "godly" intentions against them, killing their freedom and winning a significant battle. In all of this, we must go undetected, seeming inactive, if not entirely absent.

Guarding Them from Grace

Grace. We shudder at the dreadful word scattered throughout the Book. A proper understanding of grace will render any patient nearly impervious to even our finest strategies. But our experience thus far does reveal a number of ploys we can implement to dampen or even eradicate the power of grace in their lives. Here we outline three lines of attack that we have successfully utilized with a diverse range of patients.

The first is to offer them a watered-down form of grace. Have the term "grace" serve as a popular buzzword. Let them see grace as a valuable topic, even one of the most valuable. Our only real concern is to guard patients from the awareness that grace is the very *essence* of the Message itself—the gospel of grace. So encourage them to use "grace" in the names of their churches and in the lyrics of their songs. Breed such familiarity that utterance of the word itself becomes nothing but meaningless repetition for them. It will then be an innocuous "church word" tossed around casually with little or no regard for the depth of its meaning. In watering down the meaning of grace, we neutralize its power.

If this approach fails, then take a very different measure—blacken the reputation of grace. Fabricate the myth that too much grace will lead them into sin. Make them imagine that those who propose a life motivated by grace are charlatans who secretly engage in debauchery. After all, it will seem logical in their human reasoning that if they were under the radical freedom of unconditional grace, they would only take advantage, doing whatever they "want." Oblivious to the Work, these morons actually believe they *want* to sin! Thus, they expect that any measure of liberty will only reveal their supposedly wicked hearts for what they are. Remember that their pathetic view of their personhood is precisely the reason they refuse to release themselves into the splendor of the Enemy's grace. They simply will not trust their hearts, nor the Enemy who lives within them, with the outcome.

Finally, another angle we often take is that of balancing law with grace. Humans love the idea of moderation and naturally desire what they perceive as "balance" in their belief systems. So we can easily promote the notion of achieving equilibrium between law and grace. In many ways, a palatable mixture of law and grace is our ultimate ally, superior to a more law-oriented message. Why? The fact remains that pure law will eventually drive a patient to burnout, serving as his tutor to then bring him toward grace. But if a patient adopts a "healthy" balance, a law-grace mixture, he neither confronts the true stringency of the law nor experiences the pure bliss of the Enemy's grace. Instead, he settles into a felicitous middle ground that spurs human effort and strokes the fleshy ego with attainable feelings of righteousness. Herein, we offer him a vague sense that he is on the right track. This is the ultimate place for a patient to reside. So if you find the ignoramus willing, keep him there. As he continues to adopt the law-grace compromise we offer, the pure gospel of grace is veiled, and so is his most infectious freedom.

Final Thoughts

Do not let patients detect the power of grace beyond that one saving act. Do not allow them to make any connection between the Work already done and the work taking place within them.

Let them speak of grace as if it were some sort of unpredictable magic pixie dust. Do not permit them to expect the Enemy's grace to bring on upright living. Cut them off from even the faintest notion that apart from law, sin is dead. They should not see that sin loses all power over them as they are led by the Ghost in an atmosphere of liberty. If patients begin to recognize grace as the force both releasing them to be themselves *and* empowering them to live uprightly, their lives will inevitably be marked with an abject beauty and joy inexpressible.

If you witness early signs of this revelation in a patient, do not panic. Simply locate his vulnerability and employ one of the measures outlined here. Know that you will not confront any challenge that we have not already encountered. In the next chapter we expound further, detailing more nuances within the law mentality and providing specific counter-measures you can effectively take against patients' sometimes alarming choices. Rest assured that you are receiving the best possible preparation.

15

00010111+/00001000101110000111010010v./10/04010111100010100000+01110100010111000110/100010.111000101110000011-101000000

Destroy Freedom

Just as you first deceived them, so continue with them. Even if they have dismissed legalistic rules as the means to salvation, they can indeed be taught to retain a law-like system as a means to growth, a catalyst for self-improvement, or a method of pleasing the Enemy. They exchange a prison of steel for a prison of iron.

We know the ancient law is nothing more than a tutor to expose their shortcomings and thereby lead them to salvation in the One. Still, we find the humans are willing, even eager, to retain this sort of tutor after beginning their new life in him. Some of their more popular teachers even encourage the idea, and you do well to utilize them as accomplices in this regard.

It is worthwhile to note that most patients will not concede to a full-blown form of Moses. For one, they readily acknowledge the impracticality and irrelevance of the wardrobe and dietary restrictions that govern the Jewish people. But we find that if we demonstrate how they might arbitrarily select from the ancient writings a set of *moral* laws that seem most palatable, most achievable, they are generally quite amenable to the idea. The result is that some of them look to a portion of the old way, rather than to the Ghost, as both the source of and the standard for their conduct.

Thus far, we have kept a vast number of them entertained with ten commands in particular (or nine, as some exclude the seventh day ritual). The idiots pay no attention to the Book in this regard, even as it states that the ministry once etched on stone brings them only condemnation and death. They likewise disregard their own apostle Paul's account of his confrontation with the tenth of these commands ("you shall not covet") and the inevitable result—the power of sin wreaking a glorious havoc in his life.

They seem to believe that their case will somehow be different and that with the Ghost's assistance, they will surely be able to fulfill the law (or a select portion thereof). They do not even recognize the shockingly arrogant role they take on in choosing only ten or nine commands to follow, when in reality the old way of the law was an all-or-nothing proposition. Cursed was everyone who did not do everything contained in it!

So we do well to play on their choosing of nine or ten commandments, as it gives them a seemingly reasonable hope for self-improvement within the law. It is a false hope, of course. That goes without saying. But it is a hope that squelches any opportunity of experiencing the Ghost as their exclusive *source* of morality. It sustains them under the domination of sin, without them even realizing it.

Promote Spiritual Disciplines

If you cannot engage them with the old way of the law or even a select portion of it, then introduce an alternative *form* of law. We find them open to concepts such as "family values" or "Christian principles" or "spiritual disciplines." These guidelines serve as their standard and the source from which they seek to draw morality. Looking to a set of moral rules or values to live by, they shift their focus away from the Ghost. A "good" life substitutes for the grace life.

Learn from the example of Our Father Below. When faced with the first humans in Eden, what did he do? Did he merely create opportunities for them to choose evil? Not at all! In his wisdom, he knew humans were created by the Enemy to do *good*, not evil. This is their greatest weakness, as the little brutes are seduced by the allure of morality and ethics as easily as that ripe fruit slipped from the branch.

You will recall that Our Father Below, in the guise of a serpent, approached the woman and offered her the opportunity to discern good from evil, becoming like the Enemy. Remember how she leaped at the chance. She and her husband concluded that possessing the Enemy's goodness in itself was a worthy pursuit. The instantaneous effect, as you know, was separation. But the long-term effect was that with their newfound ability to "discern" good from evil, they became acquainted with self-analysis and shame. From there, mortal judgments concerning morality and ethics became an acceptable substitute for the Life.

It is no different today. We lure patients into discerning good from evil via principles and rules rather than being directed by the Life. We find that while they might begin certain practices with a natural joy in their hearts, these quickly become for them mandatory rituals and measures of spiritual "goodness." So we simply introduce unspoken standards involving frequency of study and frequency of attendance. In turn, they judge themselves, measure themselves, and inevitably feel shame as they fall short of the standards we provide them. Then, projecting their shame onto the Enemy, they assume he feels the same toward them. Consequently, he becomes the unsatisfied judge of their every move.

Morality, Not Life

Study your opponent carefully to determine which class of rules is best suited to him. A period of examination is key to identifying an appropriate plan of action. For example, some naturally gravitate toward rules such as "you must always be nice" or "you must put others first in everything." When carefully cultivated, these seemingly "good" laws can lead to extreme frustration and an unexpressed anger percolating under the surface for years. Without even realizing it, they harbor a subtle resentment toward the Enemy himself for "making" them bottle their emotions. Still others are more likely to adopt a slightly different rule such as "you must always be a good witness." This one can also be warped in inventive and entertaining ways, especially as we simultaneously work an undying criticism into the minds of their onlookers.

Indeed, there are other rules one can employ. For those studying this material within the Training College or the House of Correction, we leave this as an exercise for your ring-tailed tutors to conduct along with you. But in general, the essence of the stratagem is the following: divert a patient's attention away from the Life, centering him instead on maintaining a sense of "goodness" and avoiding evil.

We acknowledge that at first some of this might seem to you a counterproductive proposition. But any form of morality, ethics, or principled life is a harmless alternative in comparison with what might occur should they live from the Enemy's Life within. So let them serve with all their might until they are thoroughly proud of their achievements. Assist them in developing religious standards and principles.

Encourage them to live up to these in full measure, with a great sense of spiritual duty. They will live like cats chasing their own tails, around and around, as they pursue an approval they already possess.

Conclusion

Humans are naturally inclined toward, and therefore easily enticed by, rule-oriented systems. We witness the perpetual pep talks given by their ministry leaders, even telling adolescents to do more and be more for the Enemy. Then, as these young converts marry, have children, and are weighed down by normal, everyday concerns of life, they conclude they have fallen below the "radical" standard of spiritual productivity they once set for themselves.

The pinheads love to weigh their spirituality on a scale of some sort. But in this case, we tip the scales in our favor. When they feel they have met the standard set, we push them to well up with pride. When they fail, we fill them with shame. Either way, we win.

So let them fabricate a form of obedience to their rules. And let them play copycat, merely imitating the actions of a historical figure. Just do not let them *rest* in the Work and *exude* the Life.

16

000|0111+/000010001011|00001110/10001C../10/0/01011/10001010000+01||0100010111@0001110/10001U.1110001011|00011-|01000000

Destroy Funding

As you well know, the Israelites were obligated to offer a portion of their income to support the priests of old, and those priests were not permitted to earn a living by any other means. But you may not yet know that there is a line of self-appointed priests in the modern church today who mandate a specific amount from their followers. Yes, some present-day leaders essentially see themselves as a virtual continuation of that ancient priesthood. Discerning little difference between old and new, they exert a subtle form of control over their followers, setting themselves up as dispensers of blessings and strictures in the name of the Enemy. Here we are referring to their doctrine of a required 10 percent tithe.

In the panic to meet budgetary needs, some leaders essentially communicate that they do not trust their followers' hearts. Followers consequently develop a sense that they need to be steered, even manipulated, to give, because they are not otherwise inspired to freely give from a heartfelt motive.

This chapter outlines some of our best tactics with regard to the issue of their money. If you carefully heed the advice herein, you will likely succeed in your mission to kill their funding.

Money Matters

It is a most detestable sight when saints give freely of their own volition and even enjoy doing so. This is both infectious to others and detrimental to our cause. The one and only way we successfully stifle their giving is not by seeking to halt the giving itself but rather by adjusting their *motive* for giving. We simply maneuver patients toward a sense of obligation.

While the epistles written to the Body contain no instruction of any kind concerning a mandatory

10 percent tithe, many still believe in the seemingly harmless standard. We know they are free to give any amount, whether more or less. In fact, the truth is that they are free to give nothing at all! But some, perceiving little or no difference between the old way of law and the new way of grace, hold fast to a visible, tangible benchmark. (Note that the old way actually required *more* than a mere 10 percent, but as always, we find these pathetic creatures of the Enemy adopting a more toothsome form of law to mix in with their grace.)

Given their natural tendencies toward standards and measures, we find the concept of "New Testament tithing" quite useful as a perpetual catalyst for guilt. Allow us to explain exactly how we foster such a feeling within them. First, we feed patients the convoluted idea that tithing is a reliable, quantitative measure of godliness. Once they adopt this belief, they will inevitably find themselves under a cloud of condemnation. When they give anything short of 10 percent (which *will* happen), we can effectively shower them with a justifiable shame.

Note that very few actually give the percentage they feel (and publicly proclaim) is required. Our latest calculations reveal that the average giver only offers about 3 percent of their annual income, and more than half of patients give nothing at all. Ever since the 10 percent standard was put in place and enforced in their public proclamations, it has actually yielded the *opposite* of their intended effect. So we work in conjunction with the 10 percent dogma and thereby swindle them out of the pleasure of giving from the heart. Many of their own leaders pour on the guilt, aiding our cause.

Some even demand money from their congregation and guarantee the Enemy will return it twofold, sevenfold, tenfold, or more. This sets up naïve expectations that later cause patients to spiral into misery when, despite their dedication in tithing, their circumstances turn out differently from what they were promised. As the truth about these empty promises and those who perpetuate them is spread, the Message itself is maligned around the world.

Buying Blessings

Once they are firmly committed to the monetary requirement, it is only one step further for us to persuade them that the giving of money leads directly to the Enemy's blessings. Many of their world religions carry a tradition of making offerings in order to propitiate a deity or to be blessed in return, so this is an acceptable extrapolation for most patients. When they center on blessings that they expect in return, the act of giving is perverted. They fail to realize the joy that comes from giving itself.

In addition, we make it appear that the Enemy's favor can be bought like a cheap carnival trinket. Patients then readily connect dots between their giving and his blessing and assume that because one preceded the other, the former must have caused the latter. A common error among them is to assume correlation means causation. Adopting this logic, they unknowingly insult the character of their own spiritual Father. Our scheme cheats them out of the privilege of giving liberally and wholeheartedly, turning each gift into a payment due.

Conclusion

We know that the Enemy has written his desires on the lining of their hearts. He causes them to want and to do his good pleasure. He even allows them to participate in his despicable nature through the *true* knowledge of him.

Therefore, he would surely motivate them to give with both enthusiasm and generosity if only they allowed themselves to be free from the numbing sense of obligation we heap on them. So we work hard to keep them under the delusion that they cannot trust their own hearts. We rob them of the joy of cheerfully giving while not under the slightest pressure. Herein, we bolster the underlying belief that they are sinners at the core and therefore need to be led around like people of old via external requirements. In the end, they see the Enemy as someone who can be bought, rather than as someone who bought them and unconditionally showered them with spiritual riches through the One. Sometimes they can be so stupid!

17

00010111+/0000100010111000011101000010./1010V011/10001101000-0111010001011100011101000101100010111000011-101000000

Destroy Enthusiasm

*E*verything patients think and do flows from their view of the Enemy. So draw them a mental picture of the One sitting far off in the distance, frustrated at their pitiful attempts to save the world. He is weak, nearly helpless without them. If they do not act on his behalf, nothing will be accomplished. The sense that nothing can be done apart from them will fuel their tendencies toward pride or, alternatively, despair.

In so doing, you will divert them from the truth that the Enemy is not served by their human hands, as if he needed anything from them. You will awaken them to the erroneous concept that everything rests on their shoulders. And while they are in this state, you hit them with misleading notions about dedication and commitment. As we will demonstrate here, these tactics will cause them to vacillate wildly between the heights of hubris and the depths of self-loathing.

The Martyr Syndrome

Activate the Martyr Syndrome within them. Once patients see themselves as suffering servants who have "counted the cost" of true discipleship, they are effortlessly seduced by their own flattering portrait of themselves. We convince them that by their obedience, they have reserved themselves for the Enemy's special purposes. The misconception that they have qualified *themselves* for service remains fixed in their minds, and we thereby guard them from the truth that they are forever qualified by the Work alone.

Ignoring the price already paid, patients readily imagine that they must pay a price in order to participate in a "higher" life. As these losers focus on *their* obedience, they are blinded to the obedience of the One. As they seek to "die to self" and "pay the price," they turn a deaf ear to any talk of free grace. They acquiesce to the idea that some form of payment of their own is required for them to be anointed, to be filled, to be used, or to obtain whatever inventive goal they concoct. So this same payment mentality, which we once worked in Simon the Sorcerer to his demise, can be implanted in the minds of patients today. They simply refuse to believe that they have been freely given all things. They do not see that obedience comes as a *result* of their equipping, not as the means to it.

Encourage Commitment

There is nothing more discouraging to us than a patient who serves the Enemy joyfully, from the heart, free of guilt or any sense of obligation. As we have witnessed throughout the ages, this phenomenon alone can counteract years of careful planting and cultivation.

How can you prevent this? Use the strength of your opponent against him. As a patient joyfully engages in acts of service, encourage him to do more and more. Bring him to a place of such commitment that no human can joyfully sustain without "faking it." Then have him gravitate toward and obsess over only those passages in the Book that speak of service. Slide in the thought that failure to maintain his current level of effort will bring disappointment, if not consequences, from the Enemy.

At this point, a subject either tries harder or gives up. If he tries harder, we apply a deeper sense of obligation. If he gives up and walks away from the demanding "religion" of our own invention, we heap the condemnation. Either way, we succeed. And once he has chosen to try harder or give up, he will suspect correlations between his present circumstances and his current level of commitment.

As humans seem bent toward a superstitious fear of divine retribution, we can persuade them that the Enemy might smite them should he grow dissatisfied with their lack of commitment. While few will openly admit that they believe the Enemy might strike them with illness, job loss, or other negative circumstances due to lack of service, we do find many are open to entertaining this notion in the private recesses of their minds. That is all we really need—a private willingness to secretly swallow the lies we feed them.

The underlying implication in all of this is that the Enemy demands their service. If they do not meet his standard, he unleashes retribution upon their heads. He is seen not as a giver but as a taker, and an angry one at that. Rather than acting as beloved children, they ultimately feel like suffering slaves, measuring their works and wondering if they have done enough. They end up famished for the acceptance and approval they already have. Their service grows frantic and guilt-laden, and their enthusiasm wanes into despondency rather than springing from that passionate joy we vehemently abhor.

Of course, most of their leaders will not teach such obvious error in any public setting. But we certainly find them willing to *imply* it! And since their followers are already prone toward this sort of belief, they only need a gentle nudge in that direction to send them into a spiral of self-condemnation. In their humanity, they seem to nearly expect that the Enemy is angry with them and therefore must be appeased. Even though the Work was accomplished, satisfying the Enemy forever, many of the slimy snails still hold tightly to their warped view of him. We find that some never learn any different until the second death. By then, it is too late for them to notify anyone as to where they erred, and that is just the way we like it.

Urgency, Not Dependency

As they fail to operate under the love and acceptance lavished on them, they grow more and more vulnerable to our pressure tactics. They fall prey to such a sense of urgency that they are unwilling to wait on the works the Enemy has prepared in advance for them to walk in. Given the urgency to earn the Enemy's favor, to them his divine pace seems meager at best. So they find themselves forced to fabricate as many works as they can to feel they are making progress toward appeasing him.

Offer a patient convincing standards by which to measure his "growth," and he will labor endlessly under a yoke of his own making. He must not see the Life that is easy and light. Keep him working so fast and so furiously that he has no time to contemplate anything else. Then, when the patient is well on the path toward defeat, do not relax your guard. This is critical, as it is not uncommon for the Ghost to take extraordinary measures to gain a patient's attention and reverse his trajectory. So keep the patient's eyes focused on himself, that is, his lack of commitment. Shower him with accusation and offer one and only one solution: recommitment to the very ideals that have brought him to the place of despair. Have him try, and try, and try again. Even after witnessing his failures, he must be convinced that he should try once more. Pile more demands on the subject, remind him of his shortcomings, and incite him to rededicate, over and over, expecting a different outcome each time. Yes, this is the definition of insanity, but evidently it is an insanity to which they willingly ascribe.

Ensure he only sees trying, not trust; labor, not rest; dedication, not dependency. Do not allow him to equate the way he began in the Life with the way to continue. Some converts may do away with themselves in their despair; others may walk away from the fellowship of the Body; and most will in some way relegate themselves to what they believe is an ineffective life of second-tier spirituality.

There is no greater joy than to witness their demise.

18

00010111*/00001000101110000111010/100010./10/0/01011/10001010000*011101000101110000111010/100010.1110001011100011-101000000

Destroy Unity

I t has become clear that the patients' strength is in their numbers. After all, how healthy can the Body remain without its many parts functioning together as they were designed? So if you see them working as one, divide them. Prevent the formation of any united front. Each of their communities has its own unique trigger points, and over the centuries, we have learned to use these to segregate them. Take note of sensitive areas where only the tiniest bit of fuel may be needed to reignite old battles between them. Festering wounds from the past, from years or even decades ago, reopen, and a stunning sight breaks forth.

Observe their patterns of movement, as weaknesses can be easily identified with a little time and patience: by listening to leaders talking among themselves; by paying close attention to complaints received from congregants; and by eavesdropping on their loquacious gossips. In carefully examining a community's history and doctrine, you will find at your fingertips the fiery darts needed to enflame them. Sometimes just from stealthily dropping the right phrase or idea into an already fraught situation, all manner of fruit may result: broken relationships, church divisions, and even large-scale denominational schisms.

Beat Them with Baptism

First, there is the matter of baptism. Baptism is one of their public rites wherein patients are sprinkled with or immersed in water. This simple act carries importance to them in that it depicts the spiritual placement of each patient into the One. It is intended to imprint on their minds the image of their former selves dying and resurrecting through the Work. They are enveloped in the One, in union and identified with Him. The whole charade is disgusting.

We cannot allow this practice, which occurs frequently among them, to communicate anything so substantive to the masses. They can most certainly see baptism as a moment of public commitment to turn over a new leaf and reform their behavior. Or they can conclude baptism is a washing away of their sins. But if a patient goes down into the water and emerges realizing it to be a portrait of their own death, burial, resurrection, and placement into the Life, you will regret not having taken measures to prevent this. The spiritual reality portrayed in the physical act must remain hidden.

Our records indicate that one effective way to conceal the significance of baptism is to make sure they bicker over *method* rather than meaning. That is, fix their eyes on the manner of baptism rather than its significance. See to it that they debate sprinkling versus dunking, or being dunked once versus thrice. Or let them dispute whether a particular baptism performed in the past "counts" or whether another is needed to be certain. We even find some willing to posit that a baptism in *their* facility, in *their* waters, is required for acceptance into their place of worship! All of this serves as a glorious distraction. There is nothing like heated humanity—together with their slander, accusation, and judgments against one another—to keep them from a more profitable focus.

Beat Them with the Book

Second, there is the issue of the Book and its many variants. Of course, its message seems straightforward and clear to *us*. But given the evolution of human languages over two millennia, some phrases and individual word meanings are difficult for them to interpret. As a result, some patients are easily coaxed into factions as disputes of various kinds emerge over words, phrases, and even the accuracy of various translations. They engage in a subtle form of Book worship at the expense of their spiritual siblings, ostracizing those who dare read any variant of which they disapprove. The inevitable result is that they fixate on the Book. They seek to live by printed words alone, as if the text in itself holds power for change. In so doing, they ignore the living Word, the One who inhabits them. We do well to fan these flames of intellectual dispute.

Fighting Over Fate

Finally, there is the subject of fate and free will. This point of contention has a lengthy history rooted in Greek debates even before the birth of the One. Some patients are easily stimulated by idle speculations about matters of little consequence. One of the most notable of these minutiae relates to what *precisely* occurred at the moment of inhabitation: Was it their choice to receive the Life? Or was the Life thrust upon them, causing them to believe?

There is no particular side for us to take here, as we simply fuel the fire from *both* sides. It is only important that they fail to see the simplicity of the matter: the Enemy controversially fated all Gentile nations (including the Romans and Greeks of Paul's day) through his new way of the Work. Before the foundation of their world, he chose to die for the sins of the whole world, not merely those of Israel. Now any of the vile beasts can believe and be transformed.

Nevertheless, some patients today interpret the Book to say that the Enemy preselects certain individuals for salvation apart from their own choosing. Meanwhile, others vehemently defend free will, the need to call on his name. Once these discussions begin, they inevitably escalate into angry disputes and divisive factions.

At that point, both groups lose sight of more important matters, such as how to live *after* the moment of transformation. You may hear some of them even claiming that the issue of fate or free will is the one and only important doctrine from which everything else flows. Once you hear this, you know you have performed your task well, as they have shifted their attention toward irreconcilable philosophical questions above all else.

Keep a watchful eye for this opportunity, as we have already divided small communities and in fact the Body as a whole over this single issue. The matter will serve us well for decades, if not centuries, to come.

Impeding Forgiveness

In the midst of quarrels, you should not allow them to reach the place of forgiveness. You can instill within them several ideas to hinder this.

For example, convince them that forgiving someone is an emotion they must *feel* before they choose to forgive. Alternatively, persuade them it is some sort of progressive action taken little by little over time. Encourage them to believe they are not quite "ready" to forgive but may be ready soon. With this mindset, they will fail to see the *choice* of forgiveness: that it is a choosing of the will, even apart from hurt or resentful feelings. Forgiveness is then delayed, and in some cases entirely neglected.

In addition, if you persuade them that forgiveness is mainly to benefit the offender, many will withhold their forgiveness even longer as a form of punishment for the one who harmed them. But if they see that forgiveness is for their own sake as much as the offender's, they will more quickly choose it, and we will lose the foothold of bitterness we once possessed.

In summary, do not permit them to see the choice, the act of the will. If they do see the choice, do not let them know they can choose apart from how they feel. But if by some means they do decide to choose forgiveness, flood them with memories of the painful actions taken against them and feed them sensations of undeniable bitterness. Many will assume that because they still experience these flashbacks, they either cannot or did not properly forgive. Help them equate forgiveness with forgetting. As they replay the footage in their minds, they will wonder to where their resolve has vanished. They will question how they could have even presumed to forgive when clearly they have not sufficiently "dealt" with the issue.

Conclusion

In general, lose no opportunity to encourage patients to categorize, label, and dismiss one another, judging each other's views as unscholarly, less spiritual, or even heretical. In this way, they will continually harm each other and seldom join forces to live as a unified Body. They will remain alone, isolated. It is of little consequence whether they feel inferior or superior in their isolation. What matters most is to get them alone. This causes a rift in their formations and weakens their defenses. Their strength is found only in unity. Individuals are easily misled, but even entire groups of them, if they are willing to partition themselves enough times, can be easily coaxed toward biting and devouring one another.

In conclusion, it is critical to generate as much discontent among them as you possibly can. In this chapter, we focused on three frequently disputed issues (baptism, variants of the Book, and the question of fate). But it is important to note that the fundamental battle stratagems outlined herein can easily be applied to nearly any issue. If you are uncertain of how to extend your knowledge to a new context, consider inciting a dispute over musical styles or even church decor. It doesn't take much to get them started, and you will undoubtedly enjoy watching the fight.

19

00010111+-0000100010111000011101000010.101100010100011010000+0111010001011100001110100010.111000101110000011-101000000

Destroy Leaders

Of utmost importance are our efforts to penetrate the minds of their leadership, as this is by far the most efficient and effective way to reach the masses. If you focus on leaders whenever possible, these same authority figures will do the remainder of your work for you, as they transmit the very thoughts you implant in them to their own community. Note that some leaders seem naturally inclined to minister from their own experience rather than from the truths in the Book. So the ideal tactic here is to press in on leaders with delightfully demonic doctrines of our own creation. These will then be perpetuated by trusted messengers with the credibility we need. Before you know it, you will witness your own lies being presented as doctrinal truth to the Body at large. Nothing will warm your hellish heart more!

Leading Their Leaders

You may roll your eyes and sigh, thinking we are about to discuss the old chestnut of the pastor and the prostitute. It is a fact that those tried-and-true tactics to discredit and shame still survive in these times, as humans are much the same as they have always been. In this era, it is even possible to add new twists: toss in a male prostitute, for example, or add a pinch of cocaine to accompany the sex. Nevertheless, that is not what we will be detailing here. No, the strategy outlined here actually involves making leaders into "better" leaders! With this seemingly respectable goal in mind for them, we will demonstrate just how to diminish their effectiveness for the kingdom.

Even a sincere leader who dodges with ease the allure of a sexual encounter, for example, may still find himself snared like a mouse in *this* trap. Here is how it works. Many leaders already possess a desire to "better themselves to *his* glory" (at least, that is what they tell themselves!). Therefore, introduce them to the world's countless philosophies on leadership, casting vision, public speaking techniques, and business growth strategies. Of course, none of these in themselves are helpful to our cause. It is only these together with their appetite for self-improvement and for self-measuring of their impact (translation: their worth!) that will carry them off course.

So encourage leaders to train themselves and their staff members in all manner of self-enhancement. As they immerse themselves in these methods, consumed with figures and productivity, many will lose sight of the *content* of the one and only Message they are truly qualified to deliver. Instead, they will become devoted to other ideals altogether—those of self-actualization and success, however they might choose to measure them.

Make Them Compare and Despair

For many, their success will be measured in hours, numbers in attendance, and other quantifiers, or by how much popularity or praise they and their movement are gaining. Slowly and subtly, we train their minds to view and assess their ministry much like a CEO evaluates a large company, rather than functioning as discerning spiritual offspring walking in step with the Ghost.

Be sure to note the overabundance of materials—books, manuals, and seminars—full of enticing business principles with a sprinkle of "spiritual" application. Many of these will help you guide leaders along the path away from heartfelt dependency on the One. Of course, some leaders will be discouraged as they measure their ministries against a standard and fall short in their own estimation. When they begin to question their situation, whisper to them how tried-and-true their methods are, how they have guaranteed success for so many other leaders, and how the Enemy must not be "blessing" them if these same approaches did not likewise yield impressive effects for them. Some will turn on their own followers, becoming aggravated at them for the lack of "success," while others will turn on themselves.

As we foster an environment consumed with quantifiable success, neither leaders nor their followers will anchor themselves to the invaluable and immutable identity they already possess in the One.

At all costs, do not allow them to grasp the relevant meaning of the Work as it applies to their situation. They must not see the perfect sufficiency of living from their new heart, inspired by the One, letting the results be what they may. They must not grasp how intuitive and liberating walking by the internal counsel of the Ghost can be!

Induce a Sense of Superiority

Never underestimate the value of developing self-importance in them. Some leaders will think of themselves as the most important person in any room they enter. Keep pushing with these self-help, confidence-building techniques, identical to those we offer in the world.

Where possible, direct their minds toward complicated theological systems that include specialized terminology and concepts. While stimulating their intellects with the details of these systems, they will neglect the One they are designed to worship with childlike faith. Consequently, they will teach from *what* they know, not *whom* they know. Their appearance of wisdom will tickle the ears of listeners, further feeding their desire for respect from the masses. If our strategy succeeds fully, a leader is then inflated with pride, believing that knowledge is the key and that he is one of the elite few to hold that key.

Ministers and Marriage

The only thing more despicable than a solid spiritual leader grounded in the One is a stable marriage—two of them rooted in the One, tightly knit together by him. Here it is critical to divide and destroy.

Induce each marriage partner to distrust the other's motives. If they assume the worst about one other, not giving any benefit of the doubt when a difficult situation arises, their strong bond begins to loosen. Breed distrust, if not full-blown suspicion.

It is most important to prey upon them as they encounter difficulty in their circumstances. As you pit one against the other, also work to have them project into the future; this breeds worry and fear and usually paralyzes one or both of them. It also naturally brings them to the act of blaming each other.

If we successfully sabotage the marriage, we ruin the leader. So do not let them discover the goodness of the other's heart or realize that they each instinctively desire to forgive one another and live in harmony. Instead, let each regard the other as an opponent of sorts, not the grace-filled creation they truly are at their spiritual core.

Even when marriage partners discover their *own* identity in the One, do not allow them to look outside themselves and see the true identity of the one they love. If they do, the result will be a bond not easily broken.

20

00010111+/00001000101110000111011001010. /1000/0101//1000110100000+011101000101110000111011000010. 111000101110000111-101000000

Destroy the Message

You may find some leaders impervious to personal ruin. But do not be fooled into thinking this an obstacle. It is not *all* leaders (some pose no threat!) but rather the message of the Life that we must stomp out. This is best achieved as we impact their leaders early on, even while in their schools, inclining them toward a behavior focus in their public proclamations. A focus on conduct alone is a most natural inclination of the fleshly mind. Hence, a message centered on behavior modification will seem familiar, honorable, and appealing, all at the same time.

Some of you might be thinking, "That sort of 'no drinking, no smoking, no sex' pulpit-thumping preaching went out of style long ago." However, that is not what we refer to here. There are more intelligent maneuvers to employ besides droning on and on about the evils of the flesh.

You must offer a distinctive deception, and the patient must be lured by it. After all, remember that most patients resonate more with the idea of doing good, not evil. A more effective long-term approach is to give them exactly what they *think* they desire. Therefore, present them with tantalizing hoops to jump through to improve their behavior and their perceived standing with the Enemy.

Reduce Their Reading

It is imperative that leaders be convinced that their followers simply will not tolerate preaching from the Book. They must believe that patients grow bored of or disinterested in such an approach. Instead, persuade them to teach general principles like loving neighbors and being dedicated family members and servants of the Enemy. Keep their minds occupied with delivering these generic, lifeless messages found in nearly all of the world's religions. Furthermore, make sure they feel the need to fill their presentations with entertaining personal anecdotes. In their minds, the Book itself should be seen as a resource reserved for the most studious, not the population at large.

In addition, our research reveals that by casting Book study as one of their "spiritual disciplines," we lead many to assume it to be a most unpleasant act requiring rigorous effort to maintain over the long term. Note also that the term "spiritual discipline" is easily applied to their prayer as well. Now, we have no hellish idea why these children of the Enemy consider talking with their Father and reading his letters to be a "discipline." Nevertheless, they do. So promoting this concept even further works to discourage the masses from what they innately desire in their hearts—written and verbal communication with their own Father. As leaders repeatedly urge them to engage in these "disciplines," the opposite actually occurs as many patients quietly grow cold to the mandate.

Seizing Sermons

In the event that leaders search the Book in preparation for their weekly addresses, funnel their attention only toward passages concerning the *wickedness* of the world and *behavior* in the church. Without a second thought, their preaching will be consumed with "convicting" their congregation to move from bad to good behavior, with no more than a passing consideration for the Source of change.

Challenging followers to be more and do more, each and every week, is in fact the easiest form of message to deliver, as it takes little preparation. So let them perpetually speak of decision, of recommitment, of accountability, and of finding the Enemy's will and pleasing him by trying to remain in it. This will inflate the leader's ego and discourage his hearers as they perpetually compare themselves with the standard presented and fall short.

Finally, coach leaders and their followers alike to categorize and label one another in terms of spiritual achievement. There is nothing like an unspoken spiritual hierarchy to pepper a sense of both conceit and resentment throughout a community.

Finding a Focus

In some cases, you might also consider channeling leaders' efforts toward altering the political climate. We find many are willing to occupy themselves for years with attempting to reshape their civil government. Similarly, social reform seems a prominent and acceptable distraction. Take advantage of injustices we have perpetuated in the world; bring these to mind and watch as they engage in fruitless efforts that bring no lasting change, as they are nothing more than window dressing, devoid of the One.

As for those not entertained by outside causes, consume them with "growing the church," both in numbers and in programs. Keep them so occupied with building their groups and services that they have little time to consider anything else. Then, for efficiency's sake alone, they will not take time to question the quality of the message communicated within their congregations and through their programs. As long as support is coming in and the numbers look good, they'll assume they and their followers know the Message as it should be. All the while, they have grasped only the shallowest form of it.

Conclusion

Whether through a focus on church growth, behavior, or political/social reform, we can effectively recast the Message such that it is no longer about the Work. We shift the spotlight away from the One. We make the Message about them—what *they* are doing, what *they* are accomplishing, and what change *they* are bringing to themselves and the world around them. Along these lines, encourage leaders to fall in love with the *goodness* they perpetuate, and they will consequently neglect the *greatness* of the One. Their emphasis on product (behavior) rather than process (the Life) will steer them away from the divine order of the Enemy's new way.

Those who only emphasize outward signs, if they see "improvement" in congregational conduct, will believe the end justifies the means. Knowing the One as Life will become irrelevant to them once behavior appears whitewashed and reformed. So maneuver to have those who are most behavior-oriented assume leadership positions within the Body. As these leaders persistently present their "challenges" but neglect the catalyst for real, enduring growth, followers grow weary and disillusioned. Eventually, they resort to one of two responses: they begin living a life of hypocrisy, putting on a good face while feeling as if they are an utter failure; or they admit their inability to reform themselves and wallow in a self-pity. In either case, *we* are the ones who bring true reform to the church—the kind we adore.

Final Admonition

A new form of forgiveness, a newfound freedom, and a new identity—these three serve as the framework for the Enemy's new way. No patient should be permitted to piece these together, as he will inevitably perceive their power and then proclaim them to others.

A shift of focus is critical. When it comes to forgiveness, keep them fixated on *their own* work to get right and stay clean before the Enemy. They cannot turn and take notice of the Work of the One.

With regard to freedom, push them toward their many rules and induce them to feel good about themselves only when they adhere to these. Do not let them entertain even the slightest notion of resting in the Enemy's full approval.

As for their identity, they are inevitably clean and close to the One. Still, they live largely unaware of this reality. So do whatever it takes to water down the Work, so they cannot taste its effects at their spiritual core.

Keep them searching for what they already possess, diverting them away from any objective truth about themselves and the Enemy. Always blind them to the Blood, and never, ever let them see the Life.

[END OF TRANSLATION]

Andrew Farley is lead pastor of Ecclesia, an evangelical church that has resided on the high plains of West Texas for more than fifty-five years, and a bestselling author of several books, including *The Naked Gospel, God without Religion*, and *Heaven Is Now*. He serves as a faculty adviser for InterVarsity Christian Fellowship and frequently speaks at churches and university groups around the United States and in Canada. Andrew is also a professor of applied linguistics at Texas Tech University in West Texas, where he lives with his wife, Katharine, and their son Gavin.

Visit www.AndrewFarley.org for more information and free resources.

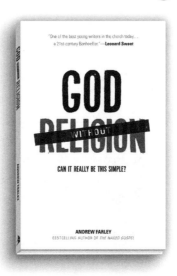

  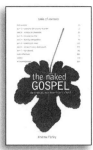